All About Madrid: A Kid's Guide to Spain's Royal City

Educational Books For Kids, Volume 31

Anam Rasheed

Published by Anam Rasheed, 2025.

ALL ABOUT MADRID: A KID'S GUIDE TO SPAIN'S ROYAL CITY

First edition. February 15, 2025.

ISBN: 979-8230951971

Written by Anam Rasheed.

Table of Contents

Prologue

Welcome to Madrid, the heart of Spain! This amazing city is full of history, art, delicious food, and exciting adventures. From grand royal palaces to lively markets, from passionate flamenco dancers to world-famous soccer teams, Madrid has something for everyone.

Imagine walking through ancient streets where kings and queens once ruled, standing in front of masterpieces by famous artists, or tasting delicious churros dipped in warm chocolate. Whether you love history, sports, music, or exploring new places, Madrid is a city that will surprise and inspire you.

In this book, you'll travel through time to discover Madrid's past, experience its traditions, and learn about the people who make this city so special. Get ready to explore secret stories, fun facts, and must-see places that will make you feel like a true Madrileño!

Let's begin our journey through Spain's royal city!

Chapter 1: Welcome to Madrid

Madrid is a city full of life, history, and excitement. As the capital of Spain, it is one of the most important and vibrant cities in all of Europe. When you arrive in Madrid, you will notice how busy and energetic it is, with people walking through the streets, enjoying delicious food, and exploring the many interesting places it has to offer. Madrid is famous for its grand buildings, fascinating museums, lively plazas, and, of course, its love for football. Whether you are interested in history, art, sports, or just having fun, Madrid has something for everyone.

One of the first things you will notice about Madrid is its beautiful architecture. The city is filled with stunning buildings that have been standing for hundreds of years. Some of them look like castles, while others have huge columns and fancy decorations. One of the most famous buildings is the Royal Palace, which is where Spain's kings and queens once lived. It is one of the largest palaces in Europe, and it is filled with golden decorations, chandeliers, and rooms that look like they belong in a fairy tale. Nearby, you will find Plaza Mayor, a large square surrounded by red-bricked buildings. This plaza has been the center of Madrid for centuries, and many important events have happened there, from royal celebrations to big markets. Today, it is a great place to sit and watch street performers or enjoy a snack at one of the many cafés.

Another thing that makes Madrid special is its museums. The city is home to some of the most famous museums in the world, filled with incredible paintings and sculptures. One of the most famous is the Prado Museum, which has artwork by some of Spain's greatest artists, like Diego Velázquez and Francisco Goya. Inside, you can see paintings that are hundreds of years old, telling stories of battles, kings, and everyday life from the past. If you like modern and unusual art, the Reina Sofía Museum is the place to go. This museum has one of the most famous paintings in the world, called *Guernica*, by Pablo Picasso. It is a powerful painting that tells the story of war and sadness, and many visitors come from all over the world to see it.

But Madrid is not just about old buildings and museums. It is also a city full of fun and excitement. If you love football, you will be thrilled to know that Madrid is home to two of the biggest football clubs in the world: Real Madrid and Atlético Madrid. Real Madrid plays at Santiago Bernabéu Stadium, a huge stadium where thousands of fans gather to cheer for their team. If you visit, you can see the field, learn about the club's history, and even sit in the same seats where the players do. Atlético Madrid has its own stadium, the Metropolitano, which is also a fantastic place for football fans. People in Madrid are very passionate about their teams, and on game days, you can hear cheers and celebrations all over the city.

Madrid is also a great place to try delicious food. Spanish food is famous around the world, and in Madrid, you can taste some of the best dishes. One of the most popular foods is *tapas*, which are small plates of different kinds of food that people share. You can try tasty things like *patatas bravas* (fried potatoes with a spicy sauce), *jamón ibérico* (a special type of Spanish ham), and *croquetas* (fried rolls filled with cheese or ham). Another famous dish is *churros con chocolate*, which are long, fried pastries that you dip into thick, hot chocolate. Many people in Madrid love to eat these for breakfast or as a snack in the afternoon.

Madrid is also a city with many green parks where people go to relax and have fun. The biggest and most famous park is called Retiro Park. It is a huge park with beautiful gardens, fountains, and even a lake where you can rent a small boat and row around. Many people come here to have picnics, ride bikes, or just enjoy the fresh air. Inside the park, there is a magical glass building called the Crystal Palace, which looks like something out of a fairy tale. It is made entirely of glass and metal, and sometimes it has art exhibitions inside. Another fun park is Casa de Campo, which is even bigger than Retiro and has a zoo, an amusement park, and a cable car that gives you amazing views of the city.

Madrid is also famous for its festivals and celebrations. One of the biggest and most exciting is *San Isidro*, a festival in May that celebrates the city's patron saint. During this festival, the streets come alive with music, dancing, and traditional Spanish costumes. People gather in plazas to enjoy concerts, eat special foods, and watch parades. Another important festival is *Three Kings' Day* in January, which is like a second Christmas for Spanish children. On this day, a huge parade goes through the city with colorful floats and people dressed as the Three Wise Men, throwing candy to the crowds.

The people of Madrid, known as *Madrileños*, are known for being friendly, lively, and welcoming. They love to spend time outside, talking with friends, and enjoying life. In Madrid, there is a special way of living called *la vida madrileña*, which means taking time to enjoy the little things, like drinking a coffee in the sun, chatting with friends at a plaza, or walking through the city at night when everything is lit up beautifully. The city never really sleeps—many restaurants and cafés stay open late, and the streets are full of people even at midnight!

Madrid is a city where history and modern life mix together perfectly. You can walk through ancient streets one moment and then find yourself in a futuristic shopping center the next. It is a place where kings and queens once ruled, but today, it belongs to the people who live there and the visitors who come to explore. Whether you want to learn about Spain's history, taste its delicious food, watch an exciting football match, or simply enjoy the energy of the city, Madrid is a place that will make you fall in love with its charm. Every corner of the city has a story to tell, and the more you explore, the more you will discover about this amazing and unforgettable place.

Chapter 2: A City of Kings and Queens

Madrid is a city filled with stories of kings, queens, and royal traditions that go back centuries. It has been the heart of Spain's monarchy for hundreds of years, and everywhere you go, you can find traces of its royal past. From grand palaces to historic streets where kings once walked, Madrid is a place where history and royalty come to life. If you have ever dreamed of visiting a city where castles, royal treasures, and legendary rulers shaped the past, Madrid is the perfect place to explore.

Long ago, Spain was ruled by powerful kings and queens who made important decisions for the country. Even though Spain still has a royal family today, their role is mostly symbolic, and the government is run by elected leaders. However, in the past, Spanish monarchs held great power, and Madrid became the center of their rule. Before Madrid was the capital, Spain's rulers lived in other cities like Toledo and Valladolid. But in 1561, King Philip II decided that Madrid should be the capital, and from that moment on, the city grew into the grand and important place it is today. He chose Madrid because of its central location in Spain, making it easier to govern the entire country.

One of the most famous symbols of Madrid's royal history is the Royal Palace, known as *Palacio Real*. It is one of the largest palaces in Europe, with over 3,400 rooms! The palace was built in the 18th century on the site of an old fortress that had burned down in a fire. When King Philip V ordered the new palace to be built, he wanted it to be as grand and magnificent as the palaces in France and Italy. Today, visitors can walk through its elegant halls and see golden chandeliers, giant paintings, and beautiful furniture fit for a king. One of the most breathtaking rooms is the Throne Room, where kings and queens once held important ceremonies. The room is decorated with red velvet, gold accents, and a ceiling painted with beautiful artwork. Another fascinating part of the palace is the Royal Armory, where you can see the shining suits of armor, swords, and shields that once belonged to Spanish kings and knights.

Even though the royal family does not live in the Royal Palace today, they still use it for special events and ceremonies. The current royal family, including King Felipe VI and Queen Letizia, lives in a smaller palace called *Palacio de la Zarzuela*, which is outside the main city. However, Madrid is still filled with reminders of Spain's monarchy. Near the Royal Palace is the Almudena Cathedral, a grand church where royal weddings and important religious events take place. It took more than 100 years to finish building this cathedral, and it is one of the most visited places in Madrid.

Madrid's royal history is also reflected in its famous plazas, or public squares. One of the most important is *Plaza de Oriente*, located right next to the Royal Palace. This plaza is surrounded by beautiful gardens and lined with statues of ancient Spanish kings. It is a peaceful place where visitors can sit and imagine what Madrid looked like centuries ago. Another famous square is *Plaza Mayor*, which was once used for royal celebrations, markets, and even bullfights during the time of the Spanish Empire.

The kings and queens of Spain were not just rulers; they were also great supporters of the arts and culture. Many Spanish monarchs loved collecting beautiful paintings, sculptures, and books, which helped Madrid become a city of art and creativity. One of the most famous kings, Philip IV, supported artists like Diego Velázquez, who painted some of the most famous royal portraits. If you visit the Prado Museum, you can see a painting called *Las Meninas*, which shows a young princess, her servants, and even the artist himself. It is one of the most studied and admired paintings in the world. Other kings and queens also helped build some of Madrid's most beautiful buildings, like the Royal Theater, where people still go to watch opera performances today.

Even though Spain is now a modern country, its royal traditions are still alive. Every year, there are special events where people can see the royal guards march in their uniforms, just like they did in the past. One of the most exciting traditions is the *Changing of the Guard* ceremony at the Royal Palace, where soldiers in fancy uniforms march in perfect formation. This event is similar to the famous guard-changing ceremony at Buckingham Palace in London. Another important royal event is Spain's National Day on October 12th, when the king and queen take part in celebrations to honor the country's history.

Madrid's royal history is also connected to the Retiro Park, one of the city's most beautiful green spaces. This park was once a private garden for the royal family, where kings and queens would go to relax and enjoy nature. It was filled with fountains, sculptures, and even a small lake where the royals could take boat rides. Today, it is open to everyone, and people still visit to walk through its lovely gardens, have picnics, and enjoy the peaceful atmosphere. The park even has a special palace called the Crystal Palace, which looks like a giant glass house and was once used for royal exhibitions.

Madrid's connection to royalty is also seen in its traditions and celebrations. One of the biggest royal events in the city's history was the wedding of King Felipe VI and Queen Letizia in 2004. The entire city was decorated for the occasion, and thousands of people gathered to see the grand procession. Another famous royal tradition is the *Royal Christmas Message*, where the king gives a speech on television every December 24th, sharing his thoughts and wishes for the country. This is an important event that many Spanish families watch together.

For those who love royal stories, Madrid is a city full of fascinating tales. Some of the kings and queens who ruled Spain were known for their bravery, intelligence, or even their unusual habits. For example, King Charles III was known as the "Mayor of Madrid" because he worked hard to improve the city, building new streets, fountains, and beautiful buildings. Another interesting royal figure was Queen Isabella II, who became queen when she was only three years old! She had a very dramatic life, and her rule was full of exciting events. Some kings, like Philip II, were known for their love of books and science, while others, like Philip V, brought new traditions to Spain from other parts of Europe.

Even though times have changed and Spain is no longer ruled by absolute monarchs, the history of kings and queens is still an important part of Madrid's identity. Whether you are walking through the halls of the Royal Palace, visiting the grand plazas where royal celebrations once took place, or exploring museums filled with paintings of past monarchs, you can feel the presence of history all around you. Madrid is a city where the past and present come together, creating a magical place where royal stories continue to inspire and amaze visitors from all over the world.

Chapter 3: The Grand Royal Palace

In the heart of Madrid, standing tall and magnificent, is one of the most breathtaking palaces in all of Europe—the Royal Palace, or *Palacio Real*. This grand building is a symbol of Spain's rich history, filled with fascinating stories of kings, queens, and royal events that shaped the country over centuries. With its enormous size, lavish decorations, and important treasures, the Royal Palace is one of the most visited places in Madrid. It is a place where visitors can step back in time and imagine what life was like for Spain's rulers as they walked through golden halls, held royal banquets, and made important decisions that changed history.

The Royal Palace is not just big—it is one of the largest palaces in the world! It has more than 3,400 rooms, covering an area of about 135,000 square meters. To put that in perspective, it is even bigger than Buckingham Palace in London and Versailles in France. The palace sits on a hill, giving it an incredible view of the city, and its grand exterior, made of stone and decorated with statues and intricate carvings, makes it look like something straight out of a fairy tale.

The story of the Royal Palace begins hundreds of years ago. Before this grand palace was built, there was an old fortress on the same spot, known as the Alcázar of Madrid. This fortress was used by Spanish kings for many years, but in 1734, a terrible fire destroyed it. After the fire, King Philip V decided that Madrid needed a new palace, one that would be grander and more beautiful than any other in Europe. He ordered the construction of the Royal Palace, inspired by the luxurious palaces of France and Italy. The new palace took many years to build, and when it was finally finished in 1764, it became the official residence of Spain's royal family.

Although Spain's modern kings and queens do not live in the Royal Palace anymore, it is still used for important royal events, ceremonies, and celebrations. Today, visitors from all over the world come to explore its magnificent rooms, each more beautiful than the last. One of the most spectacular rooms is the Throne Room, where kings once sat on golden thrones, surrounded by red velvet walls, dazzling chandeliers, and large mirrors that reflect the light, making the room glow. This is the room where important meetings and royal gatherings took place, and even today, it is used for special occasions, such as welcoming foreign leaders to Spain.

Another incredible part of the palace is the Hall of Mirrors, which was inspired by the famous Hall of Mirrors in the Palace of Versailles. This room is filled with shining chandeliers, enormous mirrors, and golden decorations that make it feel like a dream. Imagine walking through this room in the past, with kings and queens dressed in elegant clothing, surrounded by noblemen and musicians playing beautiful music. It must have been a sight to behold!

The Royal Chapel is another breathtaking part of the palace. This chapel was built so that the royal family could attend religious ceremonies without leaving their home. The chapel has high ceilings, beautiful paintings, and golden details that make it feel like a sacred and peaceful place. One of the most famous decorations inside is the fresco painted by the artist Corrado Giaquinto, which shows angels and religious figures floating in the sky.

One of the most fascinating areas of the palace is the Royal Armory, which is filled with ancient armor, swords, and shields that once belonged to Spanish kings and knights. Some of these suits of armor were worn in battles hundreds of years ago, and they are decorated with gold, silver, and intricate designs. The armory is like stepping into a real-life medieval adventure, where visitors can see how knights protected themselves in battle and what weapons they used to fight.

The Royal Palace is also home to a stunning collection of art and royal treasures. Many Spanish kings and queens were great lovers of art, and they collected paintings from some of the most famous artists in history. Inside the palace, you can find works by artists like Velázquez, Goya, and Caravaggio. These paintings show scenes from history, portraits of royal family members, and even dramatic moments from mythology. There are also grand tapestries that were handwoven with gold and silver threads, showing detailed images of battles and celebrations.

One of the most unique parts of the palace is the Royal Kitchen, which gives visitors a glimpse into how food was prepared for Spain's kings and queens. The kitchen is one of the best-preserved royal kitchens in Europe, with huge copper pots, wooden cutting boards, and old-fashioned stoves. Imagine the delicious feasts that were cooked here for grand royal banquets! The kitchen was once filled with chefs preparing roasted meats, fresh seafood, sweet pastries, and other luxurious dishes fit for royalty.

The Royal Palace is surrounded by beautiful gardens and courtyards that add to its charm. The Sabatini Gardens, located next to the palace, are filled with fountains, statues, and neatly trimmed hedges arranged in perfect patterns. These gardens are a peaceful place where visitors can relax and take in the breathtaking views of the palace. Another famous area is the Plaza de la Armería, the grand square in front of the palace, where visitors can watch the *Changing of the Guard* ceremony. This ceremony, which takes place every Wednesday and Saturday, is a spectacular display of soldiers in traditional uniforms marching in perfect formation, just like they did in the days of the Spanish Empire.

One of the most important events held at the Royal Palace is the *National Day of Spain*, celebrated on October 12th. On this day, the king and queen participate in a grand ceremony, and people from all over Spain come to Madrid to join in the celebrations. The palace is decorated with flags, and a military parade marches through the streets, honoring Spain's history and culture. Another important event is the annual reception for foreign ambassadors, where the king welcomes leaders from different countries inside the grand halls of the palace.

The Royal Palace is not just a building—it is a symbol of Spain's past, a place where history comes alive. Every room, every hallway, and every piece of art inside tells a story of the kings, queens, and important figures who lived there. From the grand throne room to the peaceful gardens, the palace is a reminder of Madrid's royal heritage and the incredible legacy of Spain's monarchy. Whether you are fascinated by history, love art, or simply want to see one of the most beautiful palaces in the world, a visit to the Royal Palace of Madrid is an unforgettable experience.

Chapter 4: The Magic of Plaza Mayor

In the heart of Madrid, there is a place that feels like stepping into a time machine, transporting visitors back hundreds of years to the days of kings, merchants, and grand celebrations. This place is *Plaza Mayor*, one of the most famous and magical squares in Spain. It is a place where history, culture, and tradition come together, making it one of the most visited and loved spots in the city. Walking through the giant archways into the plaza feels like entering a different world—one filled with stories of royal proclamations, thrilling bullfights, colorful festivals, bustling markets, and even dramatic events from Spain's past. Whether you are admiring its stunning architecture, sitting in a café enjoying delicious food, or simply soaking in the lively atmosphere, Plaza Mayor is a place where the magic of Madrid truly comes alive.

The story of Plaza Mayor begins in the 16th century, during the reign of King Philip II. Before it became the grand square we see today, the area was known as *Plaza del Arrabal*, a busy marketplace where traders and merchants sold their goods. Madrid was growing quickly, and Philip II decided that the city needed a proper central square, one that would reflect the greatness of the Spanish Empire. He hired a famous architect named Juan de Herrera, who designed a grand plaza surrounded by elegant buildings with balconies and archways. The construction continued under the rule of King Philip III, who finally completed the square in 1619. Over the centuries, Plaza Mayor became the center of life in Madrid, hosting all kinds of events, from royal ceremonies to public performances.

One of the most impressive things about Plaza Mayor is its design. The entire square is enclosed by three-story buildings with 237 beautiful balconies overlooking the plaza. These balconies were once the perfect spots for noble families to watch the exciting events that took place in the square below. The buildings are painted in warm shades of red and ochre, giving the plaza a welcoming and elegant feel. Surrounding the square are nine grand archways, known as *porticos*, which serve as entrances to the plaza. The most famous of these is *Arco de Cuchilleros*, a tall and dramatic archway with steep stairs leading into the square. The name *Cuchilleros* comes from the knife-makers who once worked nearby, sharpening and selling their blades to the butchers of Madrid.

At the center of the plaza stands an impressive bronze statue of King Philip III, riding his horse in a regal pose. This statue, which was created in 1616 by famous Italian sculptors, was a gift to the king from the Duke of Florence. It has stood in Plaza Mayor for centuries, watching over the countless events that have taken place in the square. Interestingly, for many years, the statue's mouth was mysteriously filled with small bones. When it was finally cleaned, people discovered that birds had been flying into the statue's mouth and getting trapped inside! Today, the statue is one of the most famous landmarks in Madrid, and visitors love to take pictures with it.

Plaza Mayor has witnessed some of the most important and dramatic moments in Madrid's history. In the 17th and 18th centuries, it was used for grand royal events, including coronations and public celebrations. When a new king was crowned, people would gather in the plaza to hear royal announcements, watch parades, and cheer for their new ruler. It was also a place of entertainment, where theatrical performances, jousting tournaments, and even bullfights were held. In the past, bullfights were one of the most popular forms of entertainment in Spain, and Plaza Mayor served as a perfect arena for these thrilling spectacles. Nobles and commoners alike would gather to watch skilled matadors face off against powerful bulls in dramatic battles of bravery and skill.

However, not all events in Plaza Mayor were joyful. During the time of the Spanish Inquisition, the plaza was used for *autos-da-fé*, which were public trials and punishments of people accused of crimes against the church. These events were attended by large crowds and were meant to serve as warnings to others. Although these dark moments are part of the plaza's history, they are reminders of how much Spain has changed over the centuries, moving toward a more just and peaceful society.

One of the most magical times to visit Plaza Mayor is during the holiday season, when it transforms into a dazzling Christmas market. Every December, the square is filled with little wooden stalls selling festive decorations, handmade crafts, and delicious seasonal treats. Twinkling lights are strung across the square, and a giant Christmas tree stands tall in the center, bringing holiday cheer to everyone who visits. Families come to buy nativity figurines, children run around excitedly, and the air is filled with the sweet scent of roasted chestnuts and *turrón*, a traditional Spanish almond candy. The Christmas market in Plaza Mayor is one of the oldest in Spain, and it continues to be a beloved holiday tradition for locals and tourists alike.

No visit to Plaza Mayor is complete without tasting some of the delicious food found in and around the square. One of the most famous treats is the *bocadillo de calamares*, or fried calamari sandwich, a simple yet mouthwatering dish that Madrid is known for. Many small restaurants around the plaza serve this crispy, golden sandwich, and it has become a must-try for anyone visiting the city. Another classic treat is *churros con chocolate*, crispy fried dough sticks dipped into thick, rich hot chocolate. Sitting at a café in Plaza Mayor, sipping a cup of hot chocolate and watching the world go by, is one of the most enjoyable experiences in Madrid.

Throughout the year, Plaza Mayor hosts all kinds of festivals, concerts, and special events that bring people together in celebration. One of the most exciting is *San Isidro Festival*, which honors Madrid's patron saint, San Isidro. During this festival, the square is filled with music, dancing, and traditional performances. People dress in traditional *chulapo* outfits, with men wearing checkered vests and women wearing colorful dresses with shawls. There are also parades, puppet shows, and delicious food stalls serving classic Madrid dishes. The festival is a wonderful way to experience the lively spirit of Madrid and its deep cultural traditions.

Even when no special events are happening, Plaza Mayor is always full of life. Street performers entertain crowds with music, magic tricks, and art. Artists set up their easels, painting beautiful scenes of the square. Tourists and locals alike stroll through, taking in the beauty of the plaza and the surrounding buildings. At any time of day, Plaza Mayor is a place of energy, history, and charm.

Over the centuries, Plaza Mayor has survived fires, political changes, and the passage of time, yet it remains one of Madrid's most beloved places. Whether you are visiting for the first time or returning to experience its magic again, the plaza has something special for everyone. It is a place where the past and present come together, where history is written in every stone, and where the heart of Madrid beats strong. No matter where you go in the city, the magic of Plaza Mayor will always be a part of Madrid's story, welcoming visitors with its timeless beauty and vibrant atmosphere.

Chapter 5: Madrid's Ancient Origins

Long before Madrid became the bustling capital of Spain, with its grand palaces, lively plazas, and world-famous museums, it was a much smaller and quieter place, hidden in the rolling hills of central Spain. The story of Madrid's ancient origins goes back more than a thousand years, to a time when it was just a small settlement surrounded by forests, rivers, and open plains. Unlike cities such as Rome or Athens, which were founded by mighty empires in ancient times, Madrid's history is different—it did not begin as a great city but slowly grew over the centuries into the magnificent metropolis we know today. Understanding Madrid's early history means traveling back in time to discover the people, cultures, and events that shaped its journey from a humble village to the heart of Spain.

The land where Madrid stands today has been inhabited for thousands of years. Long before Spain existed as a country, ancient peoples lived in this area, hunting animals, gathering plants, and eventually settling near rivers where they could find fresh water. Archaeologists have found evidence that humans lived in this region as far back as prehistoric times, during the Stone Age. They carved tools out of stone, painted pictures on cave walls, and built simple shelters to protect themselves from the elements. Later, during the Bronze Age, people in this region began farming, herding animals, and making pottery, showing that the area was slowly developing.

Around 2,000 years ago, during the time of the Roman Empire, Spain was known as *Hispania*, and the Romans controlled much of the land. They built grand cities like Toledo, Segovia, and Mérida, filling them with temples, theaters, and enormous stone aqueducts to bring water from the mountains. However, Madrid was not yet an important city during Roman times. Instead, it was likely just a small settlement, a place where people lived in simple houses made of wood and stone. Even though Madrid was not a major Roman city, evidence of Roman influence can still be found in the region. Roman roads passed near the area, and artifacts such as coins, pottery, and ruins of old buildings have been discovered, proving that Romans did travel through and trade in this land.

After the fall of the Roman Empire, Spain entered a period of great change. In the early Middle Ages, a group of people known as the Visigoths took control of the Iberian Peninsula. The Visigoths were a Germanic tribe who had once fought against the Romans and eventually established their own kingdom in Spain. They ruled for several centuries, building churches, fortresses, and small towns. Some historians believe that during this time, there may have been a small Visigothic village where Madrid now stands, but there is very little evidence to prove it. What we do know is that Madrid was still not a major city at this point in history—it was only after another great change in Spain that Madrid began to rise in importance.

In the 8th century, a powerful new force arrived in Spain—the Moors. These were Muslim warriors and scholars from North Africa who crossed the Mediterranean and conquered most of the Iberian Peninsula. They brought with them new knowledge, architecture, science, and ways of life that transformed Spain. It was during this time that Madrid truly began to take shape as a city. The Moors built a military fortress, or *alcázar*, on a hill overlooking the Manzanares River. This fortress was meant to protect the region from enemy attacks and served as an important lookout point because from there, soldiers could see for miles in every direction.

The name "Madrid" itself comes from the Arabic word *Mayrit* or *Magerit*, which means "place of water" or "abundant water." The Moors were skilled engineers and knew how to find underground water sources, so they built a system of wells and canals to provide fresh water to the settlement. This early *Mayrit* was a small but well-defended town, surrounded by thick walls made of stone and clay to keep out invaders.

Inside the walls, people lived in simple houses, worked in markets, and gathered in mosques for prayer.

For about two hundred years, Madrid remained under Moorish rule, but it was never as important as cities like Córdoba, Seville, or Granada, which were the centers of culture and learning in Muslim Spain. However, that changed in the 11th century when Christian kings from the north of Spain began a long and difficult campaign to take back the land from the Moors. This period, known as the *Reconquista*, lasted for centuries, with battles being fought across Spain as Christian armies slowly pushed southward.

In the year 1083, King Alfonso VI of Castile conquered Madrid, and the city became part of Christian Spain. The Moors who lived there either left, stayed and adapted to the new rule, or were forced to move to other parts of the country. The Christians built new churches, monasteries, and castles, but they also kept some of the Moorish structures and used their knowledge of water systems and agriculture. Over time, Madrid began to grow, though it was still a small town compared to larger cities like Toledo and Burgos.

During the late Middle Ages, Madrid developed a strong identity of its own. It became a place where Christian, Muslim, and Jewish communities lived side by side, sharing their customs, trades, and traditions. The city's location in central Spain made it an important stop for merchants and travelers. Markets filled the streets with traders selling fabrics, spices, and fresh produce. Farmers from nearby villages brought wheat, olives, and grapes to sell, and craftsmen made leather goods, weapons, and pottery. Madrid was not yet the grand capital of Spain, but it was beginning to show signs of becoming an important city.

A major turning point came in 1561 when King Philip II made an unexpected decision—he moved the royal court from Toledo to Madrid, making it the capital of Spain. This decision changed the course of history forever. Almost overnight, Madrid went from being a small town to the center of political power in Spain. Nobles, government officials, and wealthy merchants moved to the city, and soon, palaces, grand churches, and elegant plazas were built to reflect the city's new importance.

From that moment on, Madrid never stopped growing. It became the heart of the Spanish Empire, a place where kings ruled over lands that stretched across Europe, the Americas, and beyond. Over the centuries, it expanded into the vibrant and dynamic city we see today, filled with rich history, art, and culture.

Even though Madrid is now a modern city with skyscrapers, busy streets, and a population of millions, its ancient origins can still be found if you know where to look. The ruins of the old Moorish walls still stand in some places, reminding visitors of the city's early days as a fortress. The layout of some streets follows the paths created in medieval times, and historic buildings whisper stories of the past. Madrid's ancient origins are woven into its streets, its buildings, and its traditions, making it a city that not only embraces the present but also proudly remembers its fascinating past.

Chapter 6: Prado Museum and Its Masterpieces

Deep in the heart of Madrid, standing tall among grand boulevards and beautiful parks, is one of the most important and breathtaking art museums in the world—the *Museo del Prado*, or the Prado Museum. It is a place where history and creativity come to life, where the greatest painters of all time have left behind masterpieces that tell stories of kings and queens, battles and victories, love and sorrow, myths and legends. With over 8,000 paintings, thousands of sculptures, and countless drawings and prints, the Prado Museum is not just a museum—it is a treasure chest filled with the wonders of European art. Walking through its halls is like stepping into a giant picture book, with every painting capturing a different moment from history.

The story of the Prado Museum began more than 200 years ago, during the rule of King Charles III of Spain in the 18th century. At that time, many European countries were building great museums to display their nations' artistic achievements. The king wanted Madrid to have a magnificent museum of its own, one that would hold the finest works of Spanish and European art. His son, King Ferdinand VII, and his wife, Queen Maria Isabel of Portugal, made this dream come true. In 1819, the Prado Museum officially opened its doors to the public, showcasing some of the finest paintings ever created. At first, it was a royal collection meant to be enjoyed only by kings, nobles, and important guests, but over time, it became a museum for everyone, welcoming visitors from all over the world.

The Prado is not just a place to admire paintings—it is a place to meet the greatest artists in history. From the moment you enter, you are surrounded by the works of legendary painters like Diego Velázquez, Francisco Goya, El Greco, Hieronymus Bosch, Peter Paul Rubens, and Titian. Each room is filled with incredible paintings that reveal the artistic genius of different centuries. Some are realistic, showing everyday life with great detail, while others are full of mystery, imagination, and magic. Some paintings are enormous, covering entire walls, while others are small and delicate, meant to be observed up close.

One of the most famous and mesmerizing paintings in the museum is *Las Meninas* by Diego Velázquez. Painted in 1656, this masterpiece is considered one of the greatest paintings in the world. It shows a young princess, Infanta Margarita, surrounded by her ladies-in-waiting, a dwarf, a dog, and Velázquez himself, who appears to be painting on a large canvas. In the background, a mirror reflects the image of the king and queen of Spain, who seem to be standing outside the painting, looking at the scene. But who is the real subject of the painting? Is it the princess? The king and queen? Or is it Velázquez himself? This mysterious composition has puzzled art lovers for centuries, making *Las Meninas* a painting that invites visitors to think, imagine, and interpret its secrets.

Another remarkable masterpiece in the Prado is *The Garden of Earthly Delights* by Hieronymus Bosch. Painted in the late 15th century, this incredible triptych (a painting divided into three panels) takes viewers on a surreal journey through paradise, earthly pleasures, and the horrors of hell. The left panel shows a peaceful and beautiful Garden of Eden, where Adam and Eve stand before God. The central panel is filled with bizarre and fantastical creatures, representing human desires and temptations. The right panel, however, is dark and terrifying, showing strange monsters punishing sinners in a chaotic and eerie landscape. The painting is filled with tiny details, and every time you look at it, you discover something new—a hidden figure, an odd animal, or an unexpected scene. It is one of the most mysterious and fascinating paintings in art history, making visitors stop in wonder and amazement.

The Prado Museum is also home to many works by Francisco Goya, one of Spain's greatest and most revolutionary painters. His paintings capture the beauty, tragedy, and drama of life. Two of his most powerful paintings, *The Second of May 1808* and *The Third of May 1808*, tell the story of the Spanish resistance against the French invasion. *The Second of May* shows a fierce battle between Spanish rebels and French soldiers, with chaos and violence filling the scene. *The Third of May*, on the other hand, is even more emotional—it depicts a group of unarmed Spanish men being executed by French troops, with one man in a white shirt standing in the center, raising his arms in surrender. His face is filled with fear and courage, making this painting one of the most dramatic and unforgettable works of art in the museum.

Goya also painted the famous *Black Paintings*, a series of dark and haunting images created in the last years of his life. These paintings, originally painted on the walls of his house, show eerie and disturbing scenes, such as *Saturn Devouring His Son*, which depicts the Greek god Saturn eating one of his children. These paintings reflect Goya's fears, nightmares, and thoughts about war, death, and madness. They are very different from his earlier works, showing how an artist's style and emotions can change over time.

The Prado is not only filled with Spanish paintings—it also has masterpieces from other countries, including Italy, the Netherlands, and Flanders. The works of Titian, an Italian Renaissance painter, can be found in many rooms, displaying his mastery of color and portraiture. Peter Paul Rubens, a Flemish painter, created grand and lively paintings that capture movement and emotion, making his works stand out with their dramatic and colorful style. Some of the museum's oldest and most valuable paintings come from the 14th and 15th centuries, when artists used gold backgrounds and religious themes to create stunning altarpieces.

Visitors to the Prado can spend hours, even days, exploring its vast collection, and still not see everything. The museum has entire sections dedicated to different time periods, artists, and styles, allowing people to take a journey through the history of European art. One of the best things about visiting the Prado is that every painting has a story to tell. Some paintings show historical events, others capture myths and legends, and some simply celebrate the beauty of everyday life. No matter where you look, you will find something extraordinary.

The Prado Museum is not just a place for art lovers—it is a place for everyone. Even if someone doesn't know much about art, they can still feel the emotions in the paintings, appreciate the incredible skill of the artists, and be transported to another time and place. Every brushstroke, every color, and every detail in the museum holds a piece of history, waiting to be discovered.

For Madrid, the Prado Museum is more than just a museum—it is a symbol of Spain's artistic and cultural greatness. It is a place where the past and present meet, where visitors from around the world come to admire the incredible talent of artists who lived hundreds of years ago. Whether you are looking at a royal portrait, a dramatic battle scene, a peaceful countryside landscape, or a mystical dreamlike vision, the Prado Museum offers an unforgettable experience.

Today, the Prado continues to grow, adding new exhibitions and restoring old paintings to keep them alive for future generations. It is a place of learning, inspiration, and wonder, where young and old alike can lose themselves in the magic of art. Anyone who visits Madrid should make sure to step inside this extraordinary museum, because once you enter, you will never forget the beauty and brilliance of the masterpieces inside.

Chapter 7: Flamenco Rhythms and Dance

Madrid is a city filled with music, movement, and passion, and one of the most exciting and deeply rooted traditions in Spain is flamenco. Flamenco is not just a dance—it is an art form, a way of expressing deep emotions through rhythm, music, and movement. It is a combination of singing (*cante*), guitar playing (*toque*), and dancing (*baile*), all coming together to create a powerful and unforgettable performance. The sound of clapping hands, the quick stamping of feet, the soulful melodies of the guitar, and the haunting voices of flamenco singers make this art form truly magical. Flamenco has been part of Spanish culture for hundreds of years, and in Madrid, it is alive and thriving, with flamenco shows, schools, and festivals keeping this tradition strong.

The origins of flamenco go back many centuries. It developed in the southern region of Spain known as Andalusia, where different cultures mixed over time. The roots of flamenco can be traced back to the Romani people, also known as Gitanos, who arrived in Spain from northern India around the 15th century. The Romani people brought with them a rich tradition of music and dance, which blended with the influences of Moorish, Jewish, and Spanish folk music. The result was something completely unique—an art form filled with deep emotion, storytelling, and intensity. Flamenco was not originally performed in grand theaters or large concerts. Instead, it was born in small villages, in the homes and gathering places of families, where people would sing, dance, and play music together, expressing their joys, sorrows, and struggles through their performances.

One of the most fascinating things about flamenco is that it is not just one style—it has many different forms, each with its own rhythm, mood, and meaning. Some styles of flamenco are full of energy, with fast footwork, sharp movements, and strong beats. Others are slow, emotional, and full of longing, telling stories of love, loss, and hardship. There are dozens of flamenco styles, known as *palos*, and each one has its own unique rhythm and feeling. For example, Alegrías is a lively and joyful style of flamenco, full of happiness and playful steps, while Soleá is a deep, serious, and emotional form of flamenco that expresses feelings of sadness and longing. Bulerías is one of the most exciting and complex styles, with fast footwork and tricky rhythms that challenge even the most skilled dancers. No matter the style, every flamenco performance is filled with passion and storytelling, making the audience feel every beat and movement.

The flamenco dance is one of the most breathtaking parts of a performance. Flamenco dancers, known as bailaores (for men) and bailaoras (for women), do much more than just move to the music—they tell a story with their bodies, faces, and energy. Every step, every gesture, and every movement has a meaning. The dancer's posture is strong, with the body held tall, the arms moving gracefully, and the feet tapping rhythmically on the wooden floor. Some dancers use castanets, small hand-held wooden instruments that create a clicking sound, adding an extra layer of rhythm to their performance. Others use shawls or fans as part of their dance, creating dramatic and elegant movements. Women often wear beautiful, flowing dresses with ruffles and polka dots, which swirl and move as they dance, while men usually wear fitted pants, vests, and stylish jackets.

Footwork, or zapateado, is one of the most impressive parts of flamenco dancing. Dancers use their heels and toes to create fast, rhythmic beats against the floor, almost like a drummer using their feet. The speed and precision of flamenco footwork can be astonishing, with dancers moving so quickly that their feet seem to blur. The rhythm of the footwork follows the beat of the music, creating a strong and exciting connection between the dancer, the guitarist, and the singer.

Flamenco music is just as powerful as the dance. At the heart of flamenco is the guitar, played with a technique that is unlike any other style of music. Flamenco guitarists, known as tocaores, use a special way of strumming and plucking the strings, creating both sharp, percussive sounds and soft, flowing melodies. The guitarist must follow the dancer and singer, adjusting their playing to match the emotions and energy of the performance. Sometimes, the music is wild and fast, with dramatic flourishes, and other times it is slow and soulful, allowing the audience to feel every note deeply.

The singing, or *cante*, in flamenco is deeply emotional and often sounds almost like crying. Flamenco singers, known as cantaores, have powerful, raw voices that express deep feelings. They sing about love, loss, hardship, and hope, using traditional lyrics that have been passed down for generations. Unlike in many other styles of music, flamenco singers do not always follow a strict melody. Instead, they improvise, bending their voices to match the emotion of the moment. The singer sets the mood of the performance, and the guitarist and dancer respond, creating a conversation between music, movement, and voice.

Another important part of flamenco is palmas, or rhythmic clapping. The clapping is not just random applause—it is an art in itself. There are two types of palmas: palmas sordas, which are soft and deep claps, and palmas claras, which are sharp and loud. The clapping follows the rhythm of the performance, sometimes speeding up or slowing down to add intensity and excitement. In a live flamenco show, the audience often joins in by clapping along, becoming part of the rhythm and energy of the performance.

Madrid is one of the best places in Spain to experience flamenco. Even though flamenco originally comes from Andalusia, Madrid has become a major center for flamenco performances, schools, and festivals. There are many tablaos, or flamenco venues, where visitors can watch breathtaking performances by some of the best dancers, musicians, and singers in the world. Some of the most famous tablaos in Madrid include Corral de la Morería, Casa Patas, Cardamomo, and Torres Bermejas, each offering an unforgettable flamenco experience. In these venues, audiences can sit at small tables, enjoy traditional Spanish food, and watch as passionate artists bring the stage to life with their performances.

Flamenco is more than just a show—it is a living tradition, passed down through generations. Many flamenco dancers and musicians start learning from a very young age, practicing for years to master the complex rhythms and movements. In Madrid, there are flamenco schools where students train in dance, guitar, and singing, ensuring that this incredible art form continues to thrive for future generations.

Every year, Madrid hosts flamenco festivals, such as the Suma Flamenca Festival, where artists from all over Spain come to perform. These events celebrate flamenco in all its forms, from traditional performances to modern interpretations that mix flamenco with jazz, rock, and even hip-hop. This proves that flamenco is not just a thing of the past—it continues to evolve, inspiring new generations of musicians and dancers.

Flamenco is more than just music and dance—it is the soul of Spain. It is a way of expressing emotions, telling stories, and celebrating life. Whether performed in a grand theater, a small tablao, or on the streets of Madrid, flamenco has the power to move people, making them feel the passion, pain, and joy of this incredible art form. Anyone who visits Madrid should experience the magic of flamenco, because once you hear the rhythms, see the movements, and feel the energy, you will never forget it.

Chapter 8: The Story of Retiro Park

Madrid is a city full of history, art, and culture, but it is also home to one of the most beautiful and peaceful places in Spain—El Retiro Park. Known as *Parque del Buen Retiro* in Spanish, this vast and enchanting green space is one of Madrid's most famous landmarks, offering a perfect escape from the busy city streets. But Retiro Park is much more than just a place to relax and take a walk; it has a long and fascinating history filled with royalty, grand celebrations, artistic wonders, and even a few mysteries.

The story of Retiro Park goes back almost 400 years, when Spain was ruled by powerful kings who wanted to create magnificent spaces for themselves. In the early 1600s, Spain was under the rule of King Philip IV, a monarch who loved art, theater, and lavish parties. During his reign, Madrid was growing into one of the most important cities in Europe, and Philip IV wanted a special place where the royal family could enjoy peace and beauty away from the bustling streets of the city. The king's advisor, the powerful Count-Duke of Olivares, had an idea: why not turn part of the land outside the city into a grand royal retreat? This land, which belonged to a monastery, was soon transformed into an enormous royal garden and palace complex, filled with fountains, sculptures, and pavilions where the king and his court could enjoy leisure and entertainment.

During this time, Retiro was not open to the public—it was exclusively for the king, the royal family, and noble guests. It was not just an ordinary park; it was a place for extravagant celebrations, including theatrical performances, musical concerts, and even naval battles staged on a giant artificial lake! The king's architects and artists designed beautiful gardens, intricate pathways, and impressive buildings, making Retiro one of the most splendid places in Madrid.

However, like many things in history, Retiro Park went through difficult times. In the 19th century, Spain was invaded by Napoleon's

French army, and Madrid became a battlefield. The park and its grand buildings suffered severe damage during the war, as French soldiers destroyed much of the royal complex. Many of the luxurious palaces and pavilions inside Retiro were lost forever, and the once-private royal retreat was left in ruins. But something important happened after the war: the Spanish people wanted to rebuild and create something new. Instead of restoring Retiro as a private royal garden, they decided to turn it into a public park where everyone—not just the king—could enjoy its beauty.

From that moment on, Retiro Park became one of the most beloved places in Madrid, a green oasis in the heart of the city where people could gather, play, and relax. Over time, new features were added to the park, making it even more magical. One of the most famous spots in Retiro today is the Crystal Palace (Palacio de Cristal), a stunning glass and metal structure built in 1887. Inspired by the Crystal Palace in London, this breathtaking building was originally designed to showcase exotic plants from the Philippines, which was a Spanish colony at the time. Today, it is used for art exhibitions and is one of the most photographed landmarks in Madrid.

Another highlight of Retiro is its giant artificial lake, known as El Estanque Grande. This lake has been part of the park since the time of Philip IV, and it was once used for spectacular mock naval battles, where miniature ships were placed on the water for entertainment. Today, the lake is a favorite spot for visitors, who can rent rowboats and enjoy a peaceful ride while admiring the grand monument of King Alfonso XII, which towers over the water. This monument, built in the early 1900s, features a massive stone colonnade and a statue of the king on horseback, creating one of the most majestic sights in the park.

Retiro Park is also home to a unique and mysterious statue—the Monument to the Fallen Angel (El Ángel Caído). This sculpture, created by Spanish artist Ricardo Bellver, is one of the few statues in the world dedicated to Lucifer, the fallen angel. It depicts the moment when the angel is cast out of heaven, with his wings spread dramatically and his face filled with despair. Some people find the statue eerie, while others admire it as a masterpiece of art. Interestingly, the statue is placed 666 meters above sea level, which has led to many spooky legends about its significance!

But Retiro is not just about grand monuments and history—it is a living park, full of activity and energy. Every day, people come here to jog, cycle, roller-skate, or have a picnic. Street performers entertain crowds with music, magic tricks, and puppet shows, while artists set up stalls to sell paintings and handmade crafts. On weekends, Retiro becomes even livelier, with families, friends, and tourists gathering to enjoy the sunshine, take photos, and explore its many hidden corners.

Throughout the year, the park hosts exciting events and festivals, such as book fairs, art exhibitions, and outdoor concerts. One of the most famous events is the Feria del Libro de Madrid, an enormous book fair where authors, publishers, and book lovers gather to celebrate literature. For two weeks, Retiro Park turns into a paradise for readers, with hundreds of stalls selling books of every kind and famous writers signing autographs.

Retiro is also an important place for wildlife. Even though it is located in the middle of a big city, the park is home to many different animals, including squirrels, ducks, swans, peacocks, and even turtles! The beautiful Rose Garden (La Rosaleda) is filled with thousands of roses, blooming in a rainbow of colors during the spring and summer months. In another part of the park, there is a small but charming forest area, where people can feel like they are in the countryside rather than in the heart of Madrid.

Over the centuries, Retiro has remained one of Madrid's most treasured places. It has seen kings and queens, wars and celebrations, destruction and rebirth. From a royal playground to a public paradise, Retiro Park has transformed into the beating heart of the city—a place where people of all ages can come to relax, play, and soak in the beauty of nature. Whether someone wants to row a boat on the lake, admire breathtaking sculptures, listen to music, or simply sit on a bench and enjoy the fresh air, there is something special for everyone in Retiro.

Today, Retiro Park is not just loved by the people of Madrid; it is recognized as a UNESCO World Heritage Site, meaning it is officially considered one of the most important cultural landmarks in the world. With its rich history, stunning scenery, and endless activities, it is easy to see why this park has remained a symbol of Madrid for so many years. Whether visiting for the first time or returning again and again, Retiro Park always has something new and magical to offer, making it one of the most unforgettable places in all of Spain.

Chapter 9: Soccer Fever at Santiago Bernabéu

Madrid is famous for many things—royal palaces, world-class art museums, and delicious food—but one of the biggest passions in the city is soccer! In Madrid, soccer isn't just a sport; it's a way of life. People of all ages—kids, teenagers, parents, and even grandparents—get excited about their favorite team, and no team is more famous in Madrid than Real Madrid. This legendary soccer club has fans not just in Spain, but all over the world. And at the heart of this soccer craze is the Santiago Bernabéu Stadium, one of the most famous stadiums in history.

Located in the center of Madrid, Santiago Bernabéu is more than just a place to watch a soccer game—it is a temple of the sport, a symbol of pride for millions of fans. It is where some of the greatest soccer players in history have played, where legendary matches have been won, and where the crowd roars with excitement whenever Real Madrid scores a goal. The stadium is so important to the city that on game days, the entire area around it comes alive with fans singing, cheering, and wearing white, the official color of Los Blancos, as Real Madrid is often called.

But how did this incredible stadium come to be? The story of Santiago Bernabéu goes back to the 1940s, when Real Madrid was already one of Spain's top soccer clubs. At that time, the team played in a smaller stadium, but the club's president, Santiago Bernabéu, had a vision—he wanted to build a bigger, grander stadium that would be one of the best in the world. Construction began in 1944, and after years of hard work, the stadium officially opened in 1947. It was named after the man who made it possible, and over the decades, it grew into one of the most impressive soccer venues in history.

Today, the Santiago Bernabéu Stadium can hold over 80,000 fans, making it one of the largest stadiums in Europe. It has hosted some of the most unforgettable soccer matches in history, including UEFA

Champions League finals, World Cup games, and countless victories for Real Madrid. The energy inside the stadium is unlike anything else—when Real Madrid plays, the stands shake with excitement as thousands of voices chant in unison, waving scarves and flags in support of their team.

One of the most magical experiences for any soccer fan is watching El Clásico at Santiago Bernabéu. El Clásico is the legendary rivalry match between Real Madrid and FC Barcelona, two of the biggest and most successful teams in the world. Every time these two teams face off, the entire country stops to watch. The rivalry is fierce, with fans passionately supporting their team, and the atmosphere in the stadium is electric. Some of the greatest players in history, such as Cristiano Ronaldo, Lionel Messi, Zinedine Zidane, and Ronaldinho, have played in this legendary match, creating moments that fans will never forget.

But Santiago Bernabéu is not just about big matches—it is also a place where history comes alive. Fans can visit the Real Madrid Museum, located inside the stadium, where they can see the club's trophies, jerseys, and memorabilia from decades of victories. Real Madrid has won more Champions League titles than any other club, and their trophy collection is one of the most impressive in the world. Visitors can also take a stadium tour, where they can walk through the locker rooms, sit in the players' bench, and even step onto the field where their heroes play. For young soccer fans, standing in the same place where legends like Raúl, Iker Casillas, Luka Modrić, and Karim Benzema have played is a dream come true.

In recent years, Santiago Bernabéu has been undergoing a massive renovation, making it even more spectacular. The new design includes a retractable roof, meaning that games can be played in any weather, and an advanced LED screen system that will wrap around the stadium, giving fans an even more immersive experience. When completed, it will be one of the most modern and high-tech stadiums in the world, ensuring that Real Madrid remains at the top of global soccer for generations to come.

But what makes Santiago Bernabéu truly special is not just its size or technology—it's the passion of the fans. Madridistas, as Real Madrid fans are called, are known for their dedication. Whether the team is winning or losing, the fans never stop supporting their players. Some fans have been coming to the stadium for 50 or 60 years, passing their love for the team down to their children and grandchildren. On game days, the streets around the stadium are filled with excitement. Vendors sell team merchandise, fans gather in cafés to discuss the match, and the city pulses with energy.

Even for those who don't watch soccer often, visiting Santiago Bernabéu is an unforgettable experience. The sheer size of the stadium, the roar of the crowd, and the history in every corner make it one of Madrid's greatest landmarks. It is not just a place for Real Madrid fans—it is a cathedral of soccer, a place where dreams are made, and where the love for the beautiful game comes to life in the most thrilling way possible.

Chapter 10: The Tasty World of Tapas

Madrid is a city filled with art, history, and grand palaces, but one of its greatest treasures is something delicious—tapas! If you visit Madrid, you will hear this word everywhere because tapas are an essential part of Spanish culture. But what exactly are they? Tapas are small plates of food that people share while enjoying time with family and friends. Instead of ordering one big meal, people in Spain love to order many different tapas, placing them in the middle of the table so everyone can try a little bit of everything. It's a fun and social way to eat, making every meal an exciting adventure of flavors.

The story of tapas goes back hundreds of years, and there are many different legends about how they were invented. One popular tale says that long ago, King Alfonso X of Castile had an illness that only allowed him to eat small portions of food with wine. When he recovered, he decided that bars and taverns should serve food alongside drinks to keep people from getting too tipsy. Another story claims that tapas started when bartenders placed small slices of bread or ham over drinks to protect them from flies, and soon, customers started enjoying these little snacks so much that they became a tradition. No matter which story is true, one thing is certain—tapas have become one of Spain's most famous food traditions, loved by people all around the world.

Madrid is one of the best cities in Spain to try tapas because it has countless tapas bars serving everything from classic recipes to modern creations. Walking through Madrid's streets, you will find restaurants with lively crowds, colorful plates of food, and the delicious smell of sizzling garlic, grilled meats, and fresh seafood. The best part about tapas is that they come in so many different flavors, textures, and ingredients that everyone can find something they love.

One of the most famous tapas in Madrid is patatas bravas. This dish is made of crispy fried potatoes cut into bite-sized chunks and topped with a spicy tomato sauce and sometimes a creamy garlic aioli.

The combination of crispy potatoes and rich sauce makes it a favorite for both kids and adults. Another must-try tapa is croquetas, which are small, golden-fried bites filled with creamy béchamel sauce and ham, chicken, or cheese. The outside is crunchy, while the inside melts in your mouth, making them incredibly delicious.

If you like seafood, you will love gambas al ajillo, a tapa made with shrimp cooked in sizzling olive oil with garlic and a touch of red pepper flakes. The shrimp become juicy and flavorful, and the garlic-infused oil is perfect for dipping fresh bread. Another seafood classic is pulpo a la gallega, which is tender octopus sprinkled with smoked paprika and sea salt, served on wooden plates.

Madrid is also famous for jamón ibérico, a type of cured ham that is thinly sliced and served on small plates. This ham comes from special Iberian pigs and is aged for years to develop its rich, nutty flavor. Locals often enjoy it with pan con tomate, which is crispy bread rubbed with fresh tomatoes, olive oil, and garlic. Together, they create a simple yet mouthwatering tapa.

For those who enjoy heartier dishes, there is tortilla española, a thick, fluffy Spanish omelet made with eggs, potatoes, and onions. It can be eaten warm or cold and is often cut into small squares to be served as a tapa. Another local favorite is albóndigas, which are juicy Spanish meatballs cooked in a rich tomato sauce. They are perfect for dipping bread and are always a hit with hungry visitors.

But tapas are not just about the food—they are also about the experience. In Madrid, there is a tradition called "tapeo", which means going from one tapas bar to another, trying different dishes along the way. Friends and families gather in the evenings, moving from bar to bar, ordering a few tapas at each stop, chatting, and enjoying the lively atmosphere. Many of Madrid's most famous tapas streets, like Cava Baja and Calle Ponzano, are filled with small restaurants where people stand by the bar, sip on refreshing drinks, and share delicious bites.

Tapas culture is all about sharing, exploring new flavors, and enjoying food together, making it a unique and wonderful way to experience Madrid's culinary scene. Whether you are tasting the crispy patatas bravas, savoring a slice of jamón ibérico, or dipping bread into a sizzling plate of gambas al ajillo, each bite tells a story of Spain's rich food traditions. The world of tapas is full of surprises, and in Madrid, it is truly an unforgettable adventure!

Chapter 11: The Secrets of Puerta del Sol

Right in the heart of Madrid, where the city's streets come alive with energy, stands Puerta del Sol, one of the most famous and historic plazas in Spain. Every day, thousands of people pass through this lively square, whether they are tourists taking in the sights, locals rushing to work, or street performers entertaining the crowds. But Puerta del Sol is much more than just a busy plaza—it is a place filled with secrets, legends, and deep connections to Madrid's past and present. From royal processions to revolutions, from the famous New Year's Eve tradition to the hidden symbolism of its statues, this iconic location holds stories that have shaped Madrid into the city it is today.

One of the biggest secrets of Puerta del Sol is hidden right beneath your feet. In the middle of the square, in front of the grand Post Office building, there is a small but very important plaque on the ground known as Kilometer Zero (Kilómetro Cero). This plaque marks the starting point of Spain's national road system, meaning that all the country's major highways begin from this very spot. If you ever look at a road sign in Spain and see a distance marker, that number is measured from this exact point in Puerta del Sol! People visiting Madrid often stop to take pictures standing on the plaque, as it is a symbol of Madrid being the center of Spain. Some even say that standing on it brings good luck, especially if you make a wish while placing your foot on the marker.

Another secret hidden in plain sight is the statue of the Bear and the Strawberry Tree (El Oso y el Madroño), which is one of Madrid's most important symbols. This bronze statue stands proudly in the plaza, but many people don't realize that it represents the official coat of arms of Madrid. But why a bear and a tree? The story goes back to medieval times when Madrid was surrounded by forests filled with wild bears. The strawberry tree, or "madroño," was a common plant in the area, and together, these two symbols became closely linked to Madrid's identity. Today, people consider the statue a meeting point, and it is common to hear locals say, "Let's meet at the Bear and the Tree!" before heading out to explore the city.

Puerta del Sol has also played a key role in some of Spain's biggest historical events. In the early 19th century, when Spain was under attack by the French army of Napoleon Bonaparte, the people of Madrid fought back bravely in what became known as the Dos de Mayo Uprising of 1808. Right here in Puerta del Sol, citizens took up arms against the invaders, sparking a fierce battle that eventually led to Spain's fight for independence. Later, in the 20th century, Puerta del Sol became a place where major protests and political movements took place, shaping the country's modern democracy.

One of the plaza's most exciting and well-known traditions is its New Year's Eve celebration, which is one of the biggest in Spain. Every year, thousands of people gather in Puerta del Sol on December 31st, standing in front of the Casa de Correos, the large clock tower that dominates the square. As the clock strikes midnight, a special tradition takes place—eating twelve grapes, one for each chime of the clock. This tradition, known as "Las Doce Uvas de la Suerte" (The Twelve Lucky Grapes), is believed to bring good fortune for the new year. People across Spain watch this event live on television, making it one of the most important moments of the holiday season.

But there's another secret hidden in Puerta del Sol that many visitors don't notice—the Casa de Correos itself. This grand building, which now serves as the headquarters of Madrid's regional government, has a mysterious and dark past. During the 20th century, when Spain was under the rule of the dictator Francisco Franco, this very building was used as a police headquarters and prison, where political prisoners were held. While today it stands as a symbol of government and democracy, its history reminds people of the country's struggles in the past.

Despite its past, Puerta del Sol remains a place of joy, gathering, and celebration. It is one of the best spots in Madrid for people-watching, whether you see talented street musicians, human statues, or performers dressed as famous characters. There is always something happening here, whether it's a parade, a festival, or just the daily rhythm of life in Madrid. If you ever visit Madrid, spending time in Puerta del Sol is a must—not just to see its famous landmarks but to feel the energy and excitement that make this plaza the true heart of the city.

Chapter 12: Madrid's Festivals and Traditions

Madrid is not just a city of grand palaces, world-class museums, and delicious food—it is also a city that comes alive with colorful festivals and deep-rooted traditions. Throughout the year, the streets of Madrid fill with music, dancing, parades, and celebrations that bring people together. Some of these traditions go back hundreds of years, while others are more modern, but they all have one thing in common: they show the spirit, passion, and joy of the people of Madrid. No matter what time of year you visit, you are sure to find a festival or tradition that makes Madrid feel more magical than ever.

One of the biggest and most important festivals in Madrid is San Isidro, a celebration held every year in May to honor San Isidro Labrador, the patron saint of Madrid. This festival dates back to the 16th century, when people began paying tribute to San Isidro, a humble farmer who, according to legend, performed miracles to help the poor and bring water to the dry fields of Madrid. Today, the festival is one of the most exciting times of the year in Madrid, with processions, concerts, dancing, and traditional food filling the city. People dress in traditional chulapo outfits, with men wearing checkered vests and caps, and women wearing colorful dresses with scarves. One of the most famous events of the festival takes place in the Pradera de San Isidro, a large park where families and friends gather to enjoy a picnic with special foods like rosquillas (sweet donuts) and cocido madrileño (a rich meat and chickpea stew).

Madrid also celebrates one of the biggest and most exciting New Year's Eve traditions in Spain. Every year, on December 31st, thousands of people gather in Puerta del Sol, one of Madrid's most famous squares, to take part in the tradition of Las Doce Uvas de la Suerte, or "The Twelve Lucky Grapes." As the clock on the Casa de Correos building strikes midnight, people eat one grape for each chime, making a wish for every grape. This tradition is believed to bring good luck for the new year and is watched on television by millions of people across Spain. The excitement of counting down to the New Year in the heart of Madrid, surrounded by fireworks, music, and cheering crowds, makes it one of the most unforgettable nights of the year.

Another incredible celebration in Madrid is Semana Santa (Holy Week), which takes place in the days leading up to Easter Sunday. During this time, the streets of Madrid fill with solemn religious processions, where people dressed in long robes and hoods carry statues of Jesus Christ and the Virgin Mary through the city. These processions are accompanied by the sounds of drums, trumpets, and religious hymns, creating a deeply emotional and spiritual atmosphere. Many people gather along the streets to watch these impressive processions, which are a tradition that has been followed in Spain for hundreds of years.

Madrid is also home to some of the most exciting and colorful carnivals in Spain. One of the most famous is the Carnaval de Madrid, which takes place in February or March, just before Lent begins. This festival is known for its vibrant parades, elaborate costumes, and lively music. People dress up in creative outfits, and the city comes alive with street performances, dancing, and celebrations. One of the highlights of Madrid's Carnival is the Burial of the Sardine (El Entierro de la Sardina), a humorous tradition where a fake sardine is carried through the streets in a mock funeral procession before being buried. This event, which dates back to the 18th century, marks the end of Carnival and the beginning of Lent.

Madrid also celebrates El Dos de Mayo (May 2nd), a festival that honors the bravery of the people of Madrid during the Napoleonic invasion of 1808. On this day, there are parades, reenactments, and ceremonies to remember the uprising of Madrid's citizens against French troops. The festival is filled with concerts, performances, and cultural events, making it an exciting way to learn about Madrid's history and patriotism.

One of the most dazzling and unique festivals in Madrid is the Fiesta de la Paloma, celebrated every August in the La Latina neighborhood. This festival honors La Virgen de la Paloma (Our Lady of the Dove), and the streets are decorated with colorful paper lanterns, streamers, and banners. People dress in traditional Madrid-style clothing and dance the chotis, a typical Madrid folk dance. The celebrations last late into the night, with music, food stalls, and a lively atmosphere that makes it one of the best times to visit Madrid.

Madrid is also famous for its Christmas traditions. During the holiday season, the city transforms into a winter wonderland with twinkling lights, festive markets, and nativity scenes. One of the most magical places to visit is the Plaza Mayor Christmas Market, where stalls sell handmade decorations, sweets, and gifts. Another special tradition is El Día de los Reyes Magos (Three Kings' Day), celebrated on January 6th. On the night before, Madrid holds a huge parade called the Cabalgata de Reyes, where the Three Wise Men ride through the streets on beautifully decorated floats, throwing candy to children. On the morning of January 6th, families wake up to find presents left by the Three Kings, just like Santa Claus delivers gifts in other countries.

One of the most modern festivals in Madrid is Madrid Pride (Orgullo Madrid), one of the biggest Pride celebrations in the world. Every June or July, the city fills with rainbow flags, concerts, parades, and street parties to celebrate love, diversity, and equality. People from all over the world come to Madrid to take part in the festivities, making it one of the most exciting and welcoming events of the year.

Madrid's festivals and traditions bring the city to life, offering a beautiful mix of history, culture, and fun. Whether you're watching the grand processions of Semana Santa, dancing in the streets during San Isidro, or celebrating the New Year with twelve lucky grapes, each festival has its own special meaning and excitement. These traditions are more than just celebrations—they are a way for people to come together, honor their history, and share joy with family and friends. No matter when you visit Madrid, you are sure to experience a festival or tradition that will make you feel the true heart and soul of this incredible city.

Chapter 13: Exploring the Bustling Gran Vía

Gran Vía is one of the most exciting and lively streets in all of Madrid. It is known as the heart of the city's entertainment, shopping, and nightlife, and it is always filled with people from all over the world. This famous street is lined with stunning buildings, luxury hotels, theaters, restaurants, and big-name stores, making it a must-visit destination for anyone exploring Madrid. Whether you want to go shopping, watch a musical, eat delicious food, or simply enjoy the energy of the city, Gran Vía has something for everyone.

The history of Gran Vía goes back to the early 20th century, when the city of Madrid decided to build a modern and grand boulevard that would connect different parts of the city. Before Gran Vía was built, this area was filled with small, narrow streets that made traffic and movement difficult. In 1910, construction began, and it took several decades to complete the entire street. The project was ambitious—it required demolishing old buildings and carefully designing a street that would become the center of Madrid's urban life. Today, Gran Vía is one of the most famous streets in Spain, often compared to Broadway in New York or Champs-Élysées in Paris because of its dazzling lights, luxury shops, and grand architecture.

One of the first things that stands out when you walk along Gran Vía is its beautiful buildings. Many of them were built in the early 20th century, featuring a mix of architectural styles, including Beaux-Arts, Art Deco, and Neoclassical designs. Some of the most famous buildings along Gran Vía include the Metropolis Building, with its elegant dome and golden decorations, and the Edificio Telefónica, which was once the tallest skyscraper in Madrid and is often compared to the early skyscrapers of New York City. Another landmark is the Capitol

Building, which has a huge Schweppes neon sign that lights up the street at night, making it one of the most iconic images of Madrid.

One of the most exciting things to do on Gran Vía is shopping. The street is packed with stores selling everything from high-end fashion to affordable clothing brands. International brands like Zara, H&M, Primark, and Mango have massive flagship stores along the boulevard, attracting shoppers looking for the latest trends. But Gran Vía is not just about modern fashion—there are also stores selling classic Spanish products, such as handcrafted shoes, leather goods, and traditional fans. Some of the smaller side streets that branch off Gran Vía are also home to unique boutiques and vintage shops, where you can find rare and stylish items.

Gran Vía is also known as the Broadway of Madrid because of its many theaters and musical shows. If you love the performing arts, this is the best place in Madrid to see a spectacular musical, comedy show, or play. Some of the most famous theaters along the street include the Lope de Vega Theatre, which has hosted hit musicals like *The Lion King*, and the Teatro Rialto, where visitors can watch classic Spanish and international productions. Walking down Gran Vía at night is a magical experience, as the bright theater signs and flashing lights make the whole street look like something out of a movie.

For those who love food, Gran Vía is filled with amazing restaurants, tapas bars, and cafés. Whether you want to try authentic Spanish cuisine or international flavors, there are endless options. You can stop at a traditional tavern and enjoy a plate of jamón ibérico (Iberian ham), order churros with hot chocolate at the famous San Ginés, or have a meal at one of the many rooftop restaurants that offer breathtaking views of Madrid's skyline. One of the best things to do on Gran Vía is to find a terrace café, sit back, and watch the world go by while enjoying some delicious Spanish food.

If you want to see a spectacular view of Madrid, one of the best places to go is the Riu Plaza España Hotel rooftop. This rooftop offers

360-degree views of the city, allowing you to see the entire stretch of Gran Vía as well as other famous landmarks like the Royal Palace and Almudena Cathedral. Another great spot is the Círculo de Bellas Artes, an arts and cultural center with a rooftop terrace that is perfect for watching the sunset over Madrid.

Gran Vía is also an important part of Madrid's nightlife. When the sun goes down, the street transforms into a vibrant hub of bars, clubs, and music venues. Whether you want to enjoy flamenco performances, live music, or dance the night away in a club, Gran Vía has something for every kind of night owl. Many of Madrid's most famous nightclubs and cocktail bars can be found just a short walk from Gran Vía, making it a great place to start an unforgettable night out in the city.

But Gran Vía isn't just about fun and entertainment—it has also been a place where important historical events have taken place. During the Spanish Civil War (1936–1939), Gran Vía was heavily bombed, and some of its buildings still show signs of the damage from that period. At the time, it was even nicknamed "Avenida de los Obuses" (Avenue of the Shells) because of the intense fighting that happened there. Today, however, it stands as a symbol of Madrid's strength and resilience, showing how the city has rebuilt itself and continued to grow.

One of the best ways to experience Gran Vía is to take a walk from one end to the other, starting at Plaza de España and ending at Calle de Alcalá, near the famous Cibeles Fountain. Along the way, you'll pass some of Madrid's most famous landmarks, historic buildings, and cultural sites. It's a journey that allows you to experience the pulse of Madrid, from its historic past to its modern and energetic present.

Gran Vía is more than just a street—it is a place that captures the soul of Madrid. Whether you come here to admire the architecture, shop for the latest fashion, watch an incredible musical, or enjoy a delicious meal, you will feel the energy and excitement that make Gran Vía so special. It is a street that never sleeps, constantly buzzing with life, making it one of the most unforgettable places in Madrid.

Chapter 14: The Enchantment of El Rastro Market

In the heart of Madrid, there is a place where history, culture, and excitement come together every Sunday morning. This place is El Rastro Market, the most famous and beloved open-air flea market in all of Spain. Every week, thousands of people—locals and tourists alike—gather in the La Latina neighborhood to explore its endless rows of stalls, bargain for unique treasures, and soak in the lively atmosphere. El Rastro is more than just a market; it is a tradition that has been alive for centuries, a place where people can experience the true spirit of Madrid in its most vibrant form.

The origins of El Rastro go back to the Middle Ages, when Madrid was growing as an important city. The name "El Rastro" comes from the Spanish word for "trail" or "trace," and it is believed to have originated from the days when this area was home to butcher shops and tanneries. When the workers dragged animal hides through the streets, they left a trail—or rastro—of blood behind them. Over time, more and more merchants set up stalls in the area to sell second-hand goods, antiques, and handmade crafts, and by the 18th century, El Rastro had become a well-known market where people from all over Madrid came to buy and sell items.

Today, El Rastro covers a huge area, stretching through Plaza de Cascorro, Calle de la Ribera de Curtidores, and many side streets and alleys. Every Sunday, starting early in the morning, vendors begin setting up their stalls, filling the streets with colorful displays of clothing, jewelry, books, furniture, artwork, souvenirs, and rare collectibles. Walking through El Rastro is like entering a giant treasure hunt—you never know what you might find! One moment, you could be looking at vintage comic books, and the next, you might stumble upon a handcrafted leather bag, an ancient coin, or an old Spanish painting.

One of the things that makes El Rastro so special is its unique mix of old and new. Some vendors specialize in antiques, old books, and historic artifacts, while others sell modern fashion, quirky decorations, and handcrafted jewelry. There are also stalls offering vintage vinyl records, rare postcards, and ancient maps, perfect for collectors who love discovering hidden gems from the past. If you're lucky, you might even find a one-of-a-kind piece of furniture or a beautiful ceramic dish made in Spain's famous pottery towns.

As you walk through the bustling market, you will hear the voices of vendors calling out their best deals, the sounds of musicians playing lively tunes, and the chatter of excited shoppers. The atmosphere is electric, with people bargaining, laughing, and exploring the seemingly endless stalls. Madrid locals have a saying: "En El Rastro, si buscas bien, encuentras lo que quieras"—which means "At El Rastro, if you look well, you'll find whatever you want." Whether you're searching for a rare collectible or simply enjoying the experience, there is something magical about wandering through the market's maze of treasures.

El Rastro is also a place where local artists and craftsmen showcase their work. Many stalls feature handmade jewelry, leather goods, paintings, and sculptures, making it a great spot to buy authentic and unique souvenirs. Unlike mass-produced gifts from tourist shops, these handmade items have a personal touch, often created by the very artists selling them. If you stop and talk to the vendors, they will happily share stories about how they made their products or where they found their rarest antiques.

One of the best parts of visiting El Rastro is the chance to experience Madrid's incredible food culture. All around the market, you'll find bars, cafés, and tapas restaurants where people take a break from shopping to enjoy delicious Spanish food. One of the most traditional things to do is stop at a small bar for a plate of tapas and a glass of wine or beer. Some of the most popular dishes include tortilla española (Spanish omelet), croquetas (fried croquettes), patatas bravas (fried potatoes with spicy sauce), and bocadillo de calamares (a crispy fried calamari sandwich). Many people say that eating at El Rastro is just as important as shopping there!

The fun at El Rastro doesn't stop at the main market streets. If you venture into the surrounding alleys and plazas, you'll find even more hidden treasures. Some streets specialize in specific types of items. For example, Calle de San Cayetano is known as "The Street of Painters", where artists sell beautiful paintings and sketches. Calle de Carnero and Calle de Carlos Arniches are the best places to find rare books, old magazines, and historic documents, making them a paradise for book lovers. Plaza del General Vara del Rey is known for its selection of vintage furniture, decorative items, and antiques. Exploring these side streets can lead to some of the best discoveries, where unexpected and unique finds are waiting around every corner.

El Rastro is also a place where you can feel the multicultural side of Madrid. While it is a deeply Spanish tradition, the market also reflects the diversity of the city, with vendors selling products from Latin America, Africa, Asia, and the Middle East. You might find Moroccan lamps, Indian textiles, Peruvian crafts, or African drums, adding to the global charm of the market. Many of the sellers come from different parts of the world, bringing their cultures and traditions to Madrid's most famous marketplace.

Even though El Rastro is open every Sunday and on public holidays, it is always crowded, especially from 10 a.m. to 2 p.m., which is the busiest time. If you want to explore comfortably, it's best to arrive early in the morning, when the streets are quieter, and you have more time to browse through the stalls before the biggest crowds arrive. Since the market is so large, wearing comfortable shoes is important because you'll be doing a lot of walking!

Another important tip for visiting El Rastro is to keep an eye on your belongings. Like any busy marketplace in the world, pickpockets can sometimes be a problem, so it's best to carry bags securely and avoid keeping valuables in easy-to-reach places. That way, you can enjoy the market without any worries.

At the end of the day, a visit to El Rastro is about more than just shopping—it's about experiencing Madrid in its most lively and authentic form. It's a place where the past and present meet, where you can find a mix of history, culture, and excitement all in one spot. Whether you leave with a bag full of treasures or just memories of the fun and energy of the market, a trip to El Rastro is something you will never forget. It is a tradition that has lasted for centuries and continues to be one of the most magical and beloved experiences in Madrid.

Chapter 15: A Journey Through Madrid's Metro

Beneath the bustling streets of Madrid lies a world of speed, adventure, and history—the Madrid Metro. This underground train system is more than just a way to get around; it's a journey through time, culture, and the heart of the city itself. With over 300 kilometers of tracks and 12 main lines, it is one of the largest and fastest subway systems in the world. Whether you're a local rushing to work, a student heading to school, or a visitor exploring Spain's capital, the Madrid Metro is an exciting and essential part of life in the city.

The story of Madrid's Metro began more than a hundred years ago, in 1919, when Spain's King Alfonso XIII inaugurated the first metro line. At that time, Madrid was already a busy city, and traffic on the streets was becoming a problem. Inspired by the underground systems in London and Paris, engineers designed a railway that would run beneath the city, allowing people to travel quickly and safely without getting stuck in traffic. The first metro line was just 3.5 kilometers long, running between Cuatro Caminos and Sol, but it was an instant success! Thousands of people used it every day, and soon, the city began expanding the network, adding more stations and new lines.

Today, the Madrid Metro has more than 300 stations, making it one of the most extensive and efficient metro systems in Europe. It connects every part of the city, from the historic center to the modern neighborhoods, from the grand Royal Palace to the massive airport. It even reaches small towns and suburbs outside Madrid, helping millions of people travel easily every day. The metro is known for being clean, safe, and punctual, with trains arriving every few minutes.

One of the most fascinating things about the Madrid Metro is that every station has its own unique story and design. Some are modern and futuristic, with sleek glass walls and digital screens, while others are historic and elegant, featuring beautiful tiles, murals, and sculptures. For example, Chamberí Station, one of the original stations from 1919, was closed for many years but has now been turned into a museum, where visitors can step back in time and see how the metro looked a century ago. The station still has its old advertisements, antique ticket booths, and vintage train cars, making it feel like a journey to the past.

Another interesting station is Ópera, located near Madrid's famous Royal Theatre. Here, during construction, workers discovered an ancient underground canal that had supplied water to Madrid centuries ago. Instead of covering it up, they turned it into a small museum inside the metro station, allowing travelers to see a part of Madrid's hidden history. Similarly, at Gran Vía Station, archaeologists uncovered the remains of a medieval gate that once stood at the entrance to the old city.

The Madrid Metro is also a gallery of art. Many stations feature huge murals, sculptures, and paintings by famous Spanish artists. Some lines, like Line 8 (the pink line), have a sleek, modern look with shiny silver walls and bright neon lights, while others, like Line 1 (the light blue line), still have the traditional blue and white ceramic tiles that give the stations a classic Madrid feel. One of the most artistic stations is Paco de Lucía, which has a giant mural of the famous Spanish flamenco guitarist after whom it was named.

Riding the Madrid Metro is also an adventure because of the different types of trains. Some lines have new, modern trains with air conditioning, digital screens, and automatic doors, while others have older trains with classic wooden seats and metal handles. On certain lines, the trains are extra long, with open spaces between the cars, allowing passengers to walk from one end to the other while the train is moving!

One of the best things about the Madrid Metro is that it makes exploring the city fast and easy. Want to visit the Prado Museum to see world-famous paintings? Hop on Line 2 (the red line) and get off at Banco de España Station. Heading to the Santiago Bernabéu Stadium to see a Real Madrid soccer match? Take Line 10 (the dark blue line) straight to the stadium. If you're traveling to the airport for a flight, the metro has you covered—Line 8 takes passengers directly to Adolfo Suárez Madrid-Barajas Airport, one of the largest airports in Europe.

Even though Madrid is known for its warm, sunny weather, the metro is especially useful during the hot summer months, when temperatures can reach over 40°C (104°F). The underground tunnels stay cool and shaded, making it a great way to travel without getting too hot. In the winter, when Madrid can get chilly and sometimes even snowy, the metro provides a warm, dry place to travel comfortably.

For those who want to travel beyond the city, Madrid's metro connects to the Cercanías, a high-speed commuter train network that takes passengers to nearby towns and countryside villages. These trains are perfect for a day trip to places like Toledo, Segovia, or El Escorial, where visitors can see incredible castles, medieval streets, and stunning landscapes.

One of the most interesting things about Madrid's Metro is its hidden secrets and urban legends. Some people believe that certain stations are haunted, such as Tirso de Molina, where workers have reported hearing mysterious noises at night. Others say that there are secret underground tunnels and abandoned stations hidden beneath the city, left over from past expansions. While some of these stories may just be myths, they add to the mystery and excitement of Madrid's underground world.

Despite being over a hundred years old, the Madrid Metro continues to grow and improve. The city is always adding new lines, faster trains, and better technology to make the system even more efficient. In recent years, the metro has introduced automatic ticket machines, contactless payment systems, and digital screens that provide real-time information about train arrivals. There are also plans to expand the network even further, making Madrid's metro one of the most advanced in the world.

Traveling on the Madrid Metro is more than just a way to get from one place to another—it's an adventure through history, culture, and the energy of Spain's capital. It's a place where art meets technology, where the past meets the future, and where millions of people come together to experience the rhythm of the city. Whether you're exploring its beautiful stations, riding its fast trains, or uncovering its hidden secrets, the Madrid Metro is a journey like no other.

Chapter 16: Day Trips to Hidden Treasures

Madrid is an incredible city with so much to see, but did you know that some of Spain's most fascinating places are just a short trip away? Beyond the busy streets of the capital, there are ancient castles, medieval towns, royal palaces, and natural wonders waiting to be explored. These hidden treasures make for perfect day trips—short journeys that take you away from the city for a few hours before bringing you back in time for dinner. Whether you love history, nature, or adventure, there is a magical destination just outside Madrid that will make you feel like you've stepped into a completely different world.

One of the most famous and beautiful places to visit near Madrid is Toledo, a stunning hilltop city that looks like something from a fairy tale. Just an hour away by train, Toledo was once Spain's capital and is known as the "City of Three Cultures" because, for centuries, Christians, Muslims, and Jews lived there in harmony. As soon as you arrive, you'll see its massive medieval walls, winding stone streets, and ancient buildings that have stood for over a thousand years. The most famous landmark is the Alcázar of Toledo, a mighty fortress that has seen kings, battles, and empires rise and fall. Another must-visit spot is the Toledo Cathedral, one of Spain's most breathtaking churches, filled with golden decorations, colorful stained glass, and magnificent artwork. If you love knights and swords, Toledo is the perfect place to visit because it is famous for making some of the finest swords in the world! Many souvenir shops sell beautifully crafted swords, shields, and even armor, just like what medieval knights used to wear.

Another incredible day trip is Segovia, a city that looks like it belongs in a fairy tale. Just 30 minutes away by high-speed train, Segovia is home to one of the most impressive Roman structures in the world—the Segovia Aqueduct. Built by the Romans nearly 2,000 years ago, this giant stone bridge carried water to the city without using any cement or glue to hold it together. It's a true engineering marvel! Another magical sight in Segovia is the Alcázar of Segovia, a spectacular castle that looks like the inspiration for Cinderella's castle at Disneyland. With its tall towers, stone walls, and breathtaking views, it feels like stepping into a medieval kingdom. If you get hungry while exploring, Segovia is famous for its roast suckling pig, a dish that has been cooked in the same way for centuries in traditional wood-fired ovens.

For those who love royal history, a visit to El Escorial is a must. Located less than an hour from Madrid, this enormous palace and monastery was built by King Philip II in the 16th century. It served as a royal residence, a monastery, a library, and even a tomb for Spanish kings and queens. Walking through its grand halls, you can see ancient books, royal tombs, golden altars, and beautiful artwork. One of the most impressive rooms is the Pantheon of Kings, where almost every Spanish monarch from the past 500 years is buried. The nearby mountains make El Escorial an even more breathtaking place to visit, offering fresh air, stunning views, and peaceful gardens.

If you love castles, you will adore Manzanares el Real, a small town with one of the best-preserved medieval castles in Spain—the Castle of the Mendoza family. Just an hour from Madrid, this fortress has tall stone walls, round towers, and wooden balconies that make you feel like you've traveled back to the time of knights and kings. Inside, you can explore ancient rooms filled with armor, weapons, and historical decorations. The castle also sits next to a large natural park, perfect for hiking, picnicking, or simply enjoying the beauty of nature.

For nature lovers, the Sierra de Guadarrama mountains provide an amazing escape from the city. Just a short drive or train ride away, these mountains offer hiking trails, breathtaking views, and even ski resorts in the winter! One of the most famous hiking spots is La Pedriza, an area known for its strange rock formations, caves, and cliffs. Adventurers can explore winding paths that lead to hidden waterfalls and peaceful streams, making it a great place to relax and enjoy nature.

Another hidden treasure near Madrid is Aranjuez, a city famous for its royal palaces and stunning gardens. Less than an hour away, Aranjuez was once a spring retreat for Spanish kings and queens, who built a magnificent Royal Palace surrounded by beautiful fountains, elegant bridges, and colorful flower gardens. Walking through its grand halls, visitors can see golden chandeliers, velvet curtains, and royal carriages that once carried Spain's most powerful rulers. The town is also known for its delicious strawberries, which you can try fresh from the farms or even in strawberry-flavored drinks.

For an experience unlike any other, a trip to Chinchón is a fantastic choice. This small town, about an hour from Madrid, is famous for its circular main square, which has been used for festivals, bullfights, markets, and even movie scenes! The square is surrounded by old buildings with wooden balconies, where people can sit and watch the action below. Chinchón is also known for its delicious garlic soup and anise-flavored liqueur, both of which have been traditional in the town for centuries.

If you're looking for something more mysterious, the town of Alcalá de Henares is a fascinating place to explore. It is the birthplace of Miguel de Cervantes, the famous writer of Don Quixote, one of the most important books in history. Walking through the streets of Alcalá, visitors can see ancient universities, medieval churches, and even Roman ruins that tell the story of Spain's long and rich history. The city is also known for its storks, large birds that build their nests on top of historic buildings, making for a unique sight as you walk around.

Madrid is an amazing city, but its surroundings are filled with hidden treasures that are just waiting to be discovered. Whether you want to explore fairy-tale castles, ancient Roman ruins, royal palaces, or breathtaking mountains, there is a perfect day trip for every kind of adventurer. With just a short train or bus ride, you can step back in time, uncover incredible stories, and experience the magic of Spain beyond the capital. Each of these places adds another piece to the fascinating puzzle of Spain's history, making every journey an unforgettable adventure.

Chapter 17: Legends and Mysteries of the City

Madrid is a city full of grand palaces, historic streets, and vibrant squares, but hidden beneath its beauty are centuries-old legends and mysteries that have been passed down from generation to generation. From ghostly whispers in ancient buildings to secret underground tunnels and unexplained happenings, Madrid is a place where history and mystery go hand in hand. Many of the city's most famous locations have stories of haunted spirits, strange events, and long-lost treasures that continue to captivate both locals and visitors. Whether you believe in legends or not, these tales make Madrid an even more fascinating place to explore.

One of the most famous legends in Madrid is that of the haunted Palacio de Linares, a grand mansion located in Plaza de Cibeles. This beautiful palace was built in the 19th century by the wealthy Marqués de Linares and his wife, but behind its luxurious walls lies a chilling story. According to legend, the Marqués fell deeply in love with a woman named Raimunda, only to discover later that she was actually his half-sister. Devastated but unable to part from her, the two continued their secret relationship. Some versions of the legend say that they had a child together, but fearing the scandal, they hid the baby away or even ended its life. Since then, strange noises, ghostly cries, and whispers have been heard inside the palace, and many visitors claim to have seen the spirit of a little girl wandering its halls. The mystery of what really happened inside the Palacio de Linares remains unsolved, but it continues to be one of Madrid's most talked-about haunted places.

Another chilling mystery surrounds the House of the Seven Chimneys, located near Plaza del Rey. This 16th-century mansion is known for its unexplained paranormal activity and the ghostly figure of a woman who has been seen walking across its rooftop. The legend tells of Elena, a woman who was married to a soldier serving King Philip II.

When her husband died in battle, she was heartbroken, but soon after, she disappeared mysteriously. Some say she was murdered, while others believe she died of sorrow, but her body was never found. Years later, locals reported seeing her ghost dressed in white, wandering the house and its rooftop, looking for her lost husband. Some even claim to have heard her cries at night, adding to the eerie mystery surrounding this old mansion.

Madrid's famous Royal Palace is also said to have its own share of supernatural secrets. Built on the site of an ancient Moorish fortress, the palace has been home to kings and queens for centuries, but it is also rumored to be haunted by the ghosts of past rulers and their servants. One of the spookiest stories tells of King Philip V, who was said to be obsessed with dark omens and superstitions. He spent his final days locked away in the palace, consumed by his fears, and many believe that his restless spirit still lingers in the royal chambers. Guards and visitors have reported strange noises, flickering lights, and an eerie feeling of being watched while walking through the palace's grand halls.

The Monastery of San Lorenzo de El Escorial, just outside Madrid, is not only a stunning royal palace and monastery but also considered one of the most haunted places in Spain. King Philip II, who ordered its construction, believed it would serve as a sacred place that could protect Spain from evil forces, but many believe that the building absorbed a dark energy instead. Because it was built over an old pagan burial site, some say that the spirits of ancient souls haunt its corridors. There are even stories of a hidden room deep inside the monastery, known as "The Room of Secrets", where whispers can be heard even when no one is there. Some visitors claim to have seen shadowy figures moving through the halls, and many of the monks who once lived there believed the place was cursed.

One of Madrid's most intriguing mysteries is the hidden network of underground tunnels that supposedly run beneath the city. Some historians believe that these tunnels date back to the Moorish period when Madrid was a small fortress town in the 9th century. The tunnels were said to be used for secret escapes, smuggling goods, and even supernatural rituals. One of the most famous legends tells of a tunnel that connected the Royal Palace to a distant monastery, allowing kings and nobles to travel in secrecy. While parts of these tunnels have been discovered beneath Madrid's old buildings, many believe that more secret passageways remain hidden, waiting to be explored.

Another mysterious location in Madrid is Puerta del Sol, the heart of the city and a place filled with history. While today it is a busy square, in the past, it was the site of executions, riots, and dramatic events. Some people say that on certain nights, the spirits of those who met their fate here can still be seen wandering the square. The most famous tale is that of a headless ghost, believed to be the spirit of a nobleman who was wrongly accused and executed. His ghost is said to appear at midnight, looking for justice and frightening those who dare to walk alone.

One of the most spine-chilling legends is the story of Doctor Velasco's House, a mansion that once belonged to a famous doctor in the 19th century. According to legend, Doctor Velasco was fascinated with the idea of bringing the dead back to life, and he conducted strange experiments in his home. People in the neighborhood reported seeing shadowy figures and hearing disturbing noises coming from the house. Even today, some say that the house carries a dark presence, and many who enter claim to feel a sudden chill, as if unseen eyes are watching them.

Madrid's many legends and mysteries add a thrilling layer to its history, making it a city of both beauty and secrets waiting to be uncovered. Whether it's the ghosts of old mansions, the whispers of lost souls, or the hidden tunnels beneath the streets, Madrid is a place where the past still lingers in the present. Even if you don't believe in ghosts, these stories make wandering through the city's ancient streets and mysterious landmarks an unforgettable adventure. Who knows? Maybe one day, you'll uncover a hidden legend of your own!

Chapter 18: Wildlife and Wonders at the Zoo

Madrid is famous for its royal palaces, grand plazas, and delicious food, but it is also home to something wild and exciting—the Madrid Zoo Aquarium! Located in the vast Casa de Campo Park, this incredible zoo is not just a place to see animals; it is a world of adventure, discovery, and conservation, where kids and adults alike can come face to face with creatures from every corner of the Earth. From the ferocious roar of a lion to the gentle swim of a sea turtle, the Madrid Zoo is a place full of surprises, and every visit feels like a journey into the heart of the animal kingdom.

The Madrid Zoo Aquarium is one of the largest and oldest zoos in Spain. It first opened its doors in 1770 as the Royal Menagerie, where exotic animals from faraway lands were kept for the enjoyment of Spanish kings and queens. Back then, people had never seen creatures like elephants, giraffes, or tigers up close, and visiting the menagerie was like stepping into a fairytale. Over the centuries, the zoo grew, and by the 20th century, it had transformed into a modern wildlife park, dedicated not only to showcasing animals but also to protecting them and teaching visitors about the importance of conservation.

Today, the zoo is home to more than 6,000 animals from over 500 species, each with its own unique story. As you step inside, you are greeted by lush greenery, winding paths, and beautifully designed habitats that make you feel like you have stepped into a different part of the world. Whether you are exploring the African Savannah, the tropical rainforests, or the deep blue sea, every area of the zoo offers a new and exciting experience.

One of the biggest highlights of the Madrid Zoo is its giant pandas. These adorable black-and-white bears are some of the rarest animals in the world, and Madrid is one of the few cities in Europe where you can see them. The zoo is part of a special breeding program to help protect these endangered animals, and over the years, several panda cubs have been born here. Watching these playful creatures as they munch on bamboo, roll around, and climb trees is a magical experience, and visitors often spend hours just observing them.

Another incredible section of the zoo is the African Savannah, where you can see some of the most iconic animals of the wild, including majestic elephants, towering giraffes, powerful lions, and speedy cheetahs. The elephant enclosure is particularly impressive, as it is designed to mimic their natural habitat, complete with mud pools, shady trees, and large open spaces for them to roam. If you visit at the right time, you might even see the elephants taking a bath, playfully splashing water, or using their trunks to grab food.

Nearby, the big cat enclosures house some of the world's most famous predators, including Bengal tigers, African lions, and jaguars. Standing just a few feet away from a sleeping tiger or a pacing lion, you can truly appreciate their power and beauty. The zoo's experts often give talks about these animals, explaining their hunting techniques, social behaviors, and the threats they face in the wild.

For fans of the ocean, the Zoo Aquarium is an absolute must-see. Unlike many traditional zoos, Madrid's zoo has a massive aquarium section, where visitors can explore the mysteries of the deep sea. Inside, you'll find everything from colorful clownfish and jellyfish to massive sharks and graceful sea turtles. One of the most exciting parts is the shark tunnel, where you can walk through a glass tunnel as sharks glide silently above you, their sharp teeth just inches away. It's a thrilling experience that makes you feel like you're swimming right alongside these magnificent creatures.

But the excitement doesn't stop there! The zoo is also famous for its dolphin and sea lion shows, where these intelligent marine mammals perform spectacular tricks, leap through the air, and even communicate with their trainers. Dolphins are known for their playful personalities and incredible intelligence, and watching them interact with their trainers is both educational and entertaining. These shows aren't just for fun—they also help teach visitors about ocean conservation and the importance of protecting marine life.

One of the most fascinating areas of the zoo is the Reptile House, where you can come face to face with slithering snakes, giant tortoises, and even venomous lizards. The Komodo dragon, the largest lizard in the world, is one of the zoo's star attractions. These powerful reptiles, native to Indonesia, can grow over 3 meters (10 feet) long and have a bite so powerful that it can take down large animals like deer. Standing near their enclosure and watching them move slowly with their forked tongues flicking in and out is like stepping into a prehistoric world.

For those who love birds, the zoo has a special aviary, home to some of the most exotic and colorful birds from around the world. From the brightly colored macaws of the Amazon rainforest to the majestic eagles that soar high above, this section is filled with beauty and wonder. One of the most popular attractions is the Birds of Prey show, where falcons, owls, and hawks fly through the air, showing off their incredible speed and hunting skills.

But the zoo isn't just about seeing animals—it's also about learning how to protect them. The Madrid Zoo is deeply involved in wildlife conservation projects, working to save endangered species and protect habitats around the world. They participate in breeding programs for rare animals, rescue and rehabilitate injured wildlife, and educate visitors about the importance of protecting nature. Many of the zoo's programs focus on helping species like the Iberian lynx, the European bison, and various endangered birds.

One of the most exciting things for kids at the zoo is the petting zoo, where they can interact with friendly farm animals like goats, sheep, rabbits, and ponies. Here, children can learn about how these animals are cared for, what they eat, and how they help people in different cultures around the world.

Throughout the year, the zoo hosts special events, night tours, and educational programs, allowing visitors to experience wildlife in unique ways. During the summer, the zoo even offers night visits, where you can explore the park under the stars and see how animals behave after dark. It's an unforgettable experience, especially when you hear the deep roar of a lion echoing in the night!

A trip to the Madrid Zoo Aquarium is more than just a fun day out—it's a journey into the wonders of the natural world. It's a place where you can watch pandas play, walk alongside giraffes, dive into the depths of the ocean, and hear the calls of exotic birds all in one day. Whether you love fierce predators, gentle herbivores, playful dolphins, or mysterious reptiles, there's something for everyone to discover. It's a reminder that our planet is full of amazing creatures, and we all have a role to play in protecting them for the future. So, the next time you visit Madrid, don't forget to take a walk on the wild side at one of the most amazing zoos in the world!

Chapter 19: Modern Marvels and Skyscrapers

Madrid is often celebrated for its royal palaces, historic plazas, and centuries-old traditions, but this magnificent city is also a place of modern wonders. Over the years, Madrid has transformed into a thriving metropolis of glass towers, steel giants, and cutting-edge architecture that stands proudly alongside its historic landmarks. While the city's heart beats in its old quarters, where narrow cobblestone streets wind past medieval buildings, its modern soul shines in the sleek skyscrapers, bustling business districts, and impressive feats of engineering that make up its contemporary skyline. Madrid's modern marvels tell the story of a city that embraces both its glorious past and its high-tech future, creating a stunning blend of old and new.

One of the most striking symbols of Madrid's modern side is the Cuatro Torres Business Area (CTBA), home to the city's tallest skyscrapers. The name "Cuatro Torres" means "Four Towers" in Spanish, and these incredible structures dominate Madrid's skyline, rising above the city like futuristic sentinels. Each tower has its own unique design, and together they create a dazzling display of modern engineering. The Torre Cepsa, with its sleek glass façade, looks like a shimmering blade piercing the sky, while the Torre PwC has a curving, cylindrical shape that gives it a sophisticated and elegant appearance. The Torre de Cristal, or "Crystal Tower," is the tallest building in Madrid, standing at an impressive 249 meters (817 feet) high, and its reflective glass surface captures the sunlight, making it sparkle like a jewel. Lastly, the Torre Espacio has a twisting, geometric design that seems to defy gravity, giving it a futuristic and almost otherworldly look. These four towers are not just buildings; they are symbols of Madrid's ambition, innovation, and progress, attracting businesses, international companies, and cutting-edge technology firms from around the world.

But Madrid's modern architecture isn't just about height—it's also about creativity. Take, for example, the Puerta de Europa Towers, often called the "Leaning Towers of Madrid". Unlike most skyscrapers that stand straight, these two towers tilt dramatically at an angle of 15 degrees, making them look as if they are about to fall over! This bold and daring design makes them one of the most recognizable landmarks in the city. These twin towers are also known as the "KIO Towers", named after the company that originally developed them. When they were completed in the 1990s, they became the first leaning skyscrapers in the world, proving that Madrid was not afraid to push the limits of architectural design.

Another futuristic gem in Madrid is the Castellana 81, a skyscraper with a fascinating history. Originally known as the "Torre BBVA", this building was designed in the 1980s and became one of the first eco-friendly skyscrapers in the city. Unlike traditional glass towers that reflect sunlight, this building was constructed with reddish-colored stone panels that help regulate temperature, keeping it cool in the summer and warm in the winter. Today, it stands as a model of sustainable architecture, proving that modern buildings can be both beautiful and environmentally friendly.

Madrid's modern wonders are not just about skyscrapers; they also include breathtaking bridges and innovative urban spaces. One of the most fascinating examples is the Perrault Bridge, also known as the Arganzuela Footbridge. Designed by the famous French architect Dominique Perrault, this bridge looks like a giant, twisting metal ribbon stretching over the Manzanares River. Instead of a straight walkway, it spirals and curves, creating an artistic and futuristic effect. The bridge is not just a crossing; it is a place where people can relax, take photos, and enjoy one of the best panoramic views of the city.

Another modern engineering wonder is the Madrid Rio Project, an ambitious urban renewal effort that transformed a once-forgotten part of the city into a vibrant, green paradise. For years, the Manzanares

River was hidden beneath highways and overpasses, making it nearly invisible to the people of Madrid. But thanks to the Madrid Rio Project, the highways were moved underground, and in their place, a stunning park filled with gardens, playgrounds, bike paths, and modern sculptures was created. Now, families, cyclists, and joggers can enjoy the beautiful riverbanks, all while admiring the seamless blend of modern design and nature.

One of the most futuristic places in Madrid is the CentroCentro, located inside the Palacio de Cibeles. This grand, historic building was once the main post office of Madrid, but today, it has been transformed into a cultural and exhibition center that celebrates modern art, technology, and innovation. Inside, visitors can explore high-tech art installations, interactive exhibits, and even futuristic digital displays that show Madrid's plans for the future. On the top floor, there is a stunning glass observatory where visitors can admire breathtaking views of the city's old and new architectural wonders.

When it comes to transportation, Madrid has embraced modern technology with its state-of-the-art airport and high-speed trains. The Adolfo Suárez Madrid-Barajas Airport is not only one of the largest in Europe but also one of the most visually stunning. Terminal 4, designed by famous architects Richard Rogers and Antonio Lamela, is a masterpiece of modern design. Its wave-like wooden ceiling, supported by colorful steel pillars, gives travelers a sense of openness and fluidity, making it one of the most beautiful airport terminals in the world.

Meanwhile, Madrid's Atocha Train Station is another example of blending modernity with tradition. While the original 19th-century structure still stands, a new, ultra-modern terminal was added, allowing high-speed AVE trains to connect Madrid to cities like Barcelona, Seville, and Valencia in just a few hours. One of the most unique features of Atocha Station is its indoor tropical garden, where towering palm trees and lush plants create a refreshing and relaxing environment for travelers waiting for their trains.

Madrid's love for modern technology is also reflected in its smart buildings and urban sustainability projects. The city is constantly working on ways to reduce energy consumption, lower pollution, and make daily life more efficient. Many of Madrid's newest skyscrapers have solar panels, intelligent lighting systems, and eco-friendly designs that help reduce their impact on the environment. Additionally, the city has been expanding its network of electric buses, bike-sharing stations, and pedestrian-friendly zones, proving that a modern city can also be a green city.

One of the most ambitious projects for the future is Madrid Nuevo Norte, a massive urban development plan that aims to create a new business and residential district filled with smart buildings, futuristic public spaces, and cutting-edge technology. Once completed, this project will transform Madrid into one of the most advanced cities in Europe, ensuring that it remains at the forefront of modern innovation.

From its towering skyscrapers to its futuristic bridges, from eco-friendly train stations to high-tech cultural centers, Madrid is a city that embraces the future while respecting its past. Every modern marvel in the city is a testament to human creativity, engineering, and ambition, showing that Madrid is not just a place of history, but also a city of innovation and limitless possibilities. Whether you're admiring the shimmering towers of Cuatro Torres, walking across a spiral-shaped bridge, or catching a high-speed train to another part of Spain, you are witnessing the incredible modern face of Madrid—a city that is always reaching for the sky.

Chapter 20: Fun Facts About Madrid

Madrid is a city full of surprises, history, and hidden secrets, making it one of the most fascinating places to explore. From its royal connections to its love of art, sports, and delicious food, there are so many fun facts that make Madrid a unique and exciting city. Whether you're a visitor or someone who dreams of traveling there one day, learning these amazing facts will help you see why Madrid is such a special place. Get ready to dive into a world of incredible stories, record-breaking sites, and curious traditions that make Madrid stand out from other cities in the world.

First, did you know that Madrid is one of the highest capital cities in Europe? That's right! Madrid sits at 646 meters (2,119 feet) above sea level, making it one of the loftiest capital cities on the continent. Because of its altitude, Madrid experiences hot summers but also chilly winters, sometimes even with snow! While many people think of Spain as a country with warm weather all year round, Madrid proves that you can experience both sunny heatwaves and cold, crisp winter mornings in the same place.

Another fun fact is that Madrid is right in the center of Spain—literally! There is a famous spot in the city called Kilómetro Cero (Kilometer Zero), which is the exact point from which all distances in Spain are measured. If you visit Puerta del Sol, one of Madrid's most famous squares, you can find a special plaque on the ground marking Kilómetro Cero. People love taking pictures here because it means they are standing at the official starting point of Spain's road network. Some say that if you touch the plaque, it brings good luck and ensures that you will return to Madrid one day.

Madrid is also home to one of the oldest restaurants in the world. Sobrino de Botín, located near Plaza Mayor, has been serving delicious food since 1725, making it the oldest continuously operating restaurant in the world, according to the Guinness Book of World Records! Famous writer Ernest Hemingway was a huge fan of this place and even mentioned it in his book *The Sun Also Rises*. The restaurant is especially known for its roast suckling pig, which is cooked in a wood-fired oven that has been in use for nearly 300 years. Imagine eating a meal in the same place where famous writers, kings, and travelers from centuries past have dined!

Speaking of food, did you know that Madrid is famous for a chocolatey breakfast tradition? One of the city's most beloved treats is churros con chocolate. People in Madrid love dipping crispy, golden churros into thick, rich hot chocolate, especially for breakfast or as a late-night snack. There are many places where you can try this sweet delight, but one of the most famous is Chocolatería San Ginés, which has been serving churros and chocolate since 1894! The best part? It's open 24 hours a day, so you can enjoy this delicious treat at any time—morning, noon, or even in the middle of the night!

Madrid is not just about food—it is also one of the most artistic cities in the world. The city is home to the Prado Museum, which has one of the largest and most valuable art collections on the planet. Inside, you can find masterpieces by famous painters like Diego Velázquez, Francisco Goya, and El Greco. But here's a fun fact—Madrid is also home to a mystery painting that people love to talk about. It's called "The Colossus", and for many years, it was believed to be painted by Goya. However, experts later discovered that it was not actually painted by him, and to this day, the true artist remains unknown!

One of the most fascinating landmarks in Madrid is actually from Egypt! That's right—Madrid is home to an ancient Egyptian temple called the Temple of Debod. This incredible monument was built over 2,000 years ago and originally stood in Egypt near the Nile River. In the 1960s, when Egypt needed help saving its ancient temples from flooding, Spain offered assistance. As a thank-you gift, Egypt gave Spain this incredible temple, which was carefully transported block by block and rebuilt in Madrid. Today, it sits on a hill in the city, offering one of the best sunset views in all of Madrid.

Madrid is also a city of music and dance, and one of its greatest cultural treasures is flamenco. This passionate, dramatic dance is famous all over the world, and Madrid is one of the best places to see it performed live. What makes flamenco special is that it is not just dancing—it is a powerful mix of singing, guitar playing, clapping, and stomping. If you want to experience the true soul of Madrid, watching a live flamenco show in one of the city's many tablaos (flamenco venues) is an unforgettable experience.

Madrid is also home to one of the most famous soccer teams in the world—Real Madrid! This team has won more Champions League titles than any other club in Europe and has had some of the greatest soccer players of all time, including Cristiano Ronaldo, Zinedine Zidane, and Alfredo Di Stéfano. Their home stadium, the Santiago Bernabéu, is a must-visit for any soccer fan, and it is so big that it can hold over 80,000 fans. But did you know that Madrid also has another world-famous soccer team? Atlético Madrid, Real Madrid's biggest rival, has its own incredible stadium called the Cívitas Metropolitano. When these two teams face off, the entire city is filled with soccer fever, and the match is called El Derbi Madrileño.

One of the strangest traditions in Madrid happens every year on December 31st. On New Year's Eve, thousands of people gather in Puerta del Sol, where they take part in the famous "12 Grapes of Luck" tradition. As the clock strikes midnight, people eat one grape for each of the 12 chimes, trying to finish them all before the last bell rings. If you manage to eat all 12 grapes in time, it is said that you will have good luck for the entire year! This fun and slightly tricky tradition has been followed for over a century, and it's one of the best ways to celebrate the New Year in Spain.

Madrid also has a connection to one of the most famous fictional characters ever—Don Quixote! This legendary character, created by Spanish writer Miguel de Cervantes, is one of the most famous figures in world literature. In the heart of Madrid, you can find a huge statue of

Don Quixote and his loyal companion, Sancho Panza, located in Plaza de España. People love taking pictures with these two beloved characters, who have been inspiring readers for over 400 years.

Whether it's the city's love for soccer, its world-famous art, its record-breaking restaurants, or its unusual traditions, Madrid is full of incredible fun facts that make it one of the most exciting cities in the world. Every street, every plaza, and every building has a story to tell, making Madrid a place of endless discovery and adventure. If you ever visit, keep your eyes open—you might just find another fun fact to add to the list!

Epilogue

Now that you've explored Madrid, you can see why it's such a special place! From the grand Royal Palace to the lively streets of Gran Vía, from delicious tapas to the roar of the Santiago Bernabéu stadium, Madrid is a city full of history, excitement, and adventure.

But the journey doesn't have to end here! Whether you visit Madrid in person or continue to explore through books, there is always something new to discover. Maybe one day, you'll stroll through the beautiful Retiro Park, watch a flamenco performance, or stand in front of a masterpiece at the Prado Museum.

Madrid is a city that welcomes visitors with open arms, and now, you know its secrets. Keep exploring, stay curious, and never stop learning about the amazing places in our world.

The End.

www.ingramcontent.com/pod-product-compliance
Ingram Content Group UK Ltd.
Pitfield, Milton Keynes, MK11 3LW, UK
UKHW010622060925
7762UKWH00001B/38

9 798230 951971